180 VEGETARIAN INDIAN RECIPES

180 VEGETARIAN INDIAN RECIPES

TEMPTING IDEAS FOR SOUPS AND APPETIZERS, MAIN COURSES, RICE AND LENTIL DISHES, SALADS, RELISHES, BREADS, DESSERTS AND DRINKS, WITH 180 PHOTOGRAPHS

SHEHZAD HUSAIN & RAFI FERNANDEZ

southwater

This edition is published by Southwater,
an imprint of Anness Publishing Ltd,
Blaby Road,
Wigston,
Leicestershire LE18 4SE;

info@anness.com
www.southwaterbooks.com;
www.annesspublishing.com

If you like the images in this book and would like to investigate
using them for publishing, promotions or advertising, please visit
our website www.practicalpictures.com for more information.

Publisher: Joanna Lorenz
Senior Editor: Felicity Forster
Additional recipes: Mridula Baljekar, Becky Johnson,
    Manisha Kanani, Sallie Morris and Deh-Ta Hsiung
Cover Design: Nigel Partridge
Proofreading Manager: Lindsay Zamponi
Production Controller: Christine Ni

PUBLISHER'S NOTE
Although the advice and information in this book are believed to be
accurate and true at the time of going to press, neither the authors
nor the publisher can accept any legal responsibility or liability for any
errors or omissions that may have been made nor for any inaccuracies
nor for any loss, harm or injury that comes about from following
instructions or advice in this book.

Previously published as part of a larger volume,
500 Indian Recipes

Main front cover image shows Spicy Potatoes and
Cauliflower – for recipe, see page 47.

ETHICAL TRADING POLICY
    At Anness Publishing we believe that business should be conducted
in an ethical and ecologically sustainable way, with respect for the
environment and a proper regard to the replacement of the natural
resources we employ.
    As a publisher, we use a lot of wood pulp to make high-quality
paper for printing, and that wood commonly comes from spruce trees.
We are therefore currently growing more than 750,000 trees in three
Scottish forest plantations: Berrymoss (130 hectares/320 acres),
West Touxhill (125 hectares/305 acres) and Deveron Forest
(75 hectares/185 acres). The forests we manage contain more than
3.5 times the number of trees employed each year in making paper
for the books we manufacture.
    Because of this ongoing ecological investment programme, you, as our
customer, can have the pleasure and reassurance of knowing that a
tree is being cultivated on your behalf to naturally replace the materials
used to make the book you are holding.
    Our forestry programme is run in accordance with the UK
Woodland Assurance Scheme (UKWAS) and will be certified
by the internationally recognized Forest Stewardship Council (FSC).
The FSC is a non-government organization dedicated to promoting
responsible management of the world's forests. Certification ensures
forests are managed in an environmentally sustainable and socially
responsible way. For further information about this scheme, go to
www.annesspublishing.com/trees

NOTES
Bracketed terms are intended for American readers.
    For all recipes, quantities are given in both metric and imperial
measures and, where appropriate, in standard cups and spoons.
Follow one set of measures, but not a mixture, because they are
not interchangeable.
    Standard spoon and cup measures are level. 1 tsp = 5ml,
1 tbsp = 15ml, 1 cup = 250ml/8fl oz.
    Australian standard tablespoons are 20ml. Australian readers
should use 3 tsp in place of 1 tbsp for measuring small quantities.
    American pints are 16fl oz/2 cups. American readers should use
20fl oz/2.5 cups in place of 1 pint when measuring liquids.
    Electric oven temperatures in this book are for conventional ovens.
When using a fan oven, the temperature will probably need to be
reduced by about 10–20°C/20–40°F. Since ovens vary, you should
check with your manufacturer's instruction book for guidance.
    The nutritional analysis given for each recipe is calculated per
portion (i.e. serving or item), unless otherwise stated. If the recipe
gives a range, such as Serves 4–6, then the nutritional analysis will
be for the smaller portion size, i.e. 6 servings. The analysis does not
include optional ingredients, such as salt added to taste.
    Medium (US large) eggs are used unless otherwise stated.

Contents

Introduction

India is home to one of the most popular and exciting cuisines in the world. Indian food is epitomized by brightly coloured vegetables in richly flavoured sauces, nutty-flavoured beans and lentils, and, of course, an array of spices that warm the body and soothe the spirit. Many Indian people are vegetarian, so there is no

shortage of delectable recipes that utilize nuts, beans, peas, rice, lentils and fruit, making substantial and nutritious meals that are guaranteed to appeal. Food enthusiasts have a wealth of choice when it comes to adventurous vegetarian cooking – if you enjoy creating tasty Indian food, look no further than this volume for a wonderful selection of exciting vegetable-based recipes. In these pages there are simple, quick-and-easy dishes, as well as more complex recipes that involve blending aromatic spices and flavourings to achieve a truly authentic taste of the East.

The beauty of Indian cooking is in its variety. Different areas and traditions have developed their own regional specialities, and recipes have been handed down through the generations as various combinations of textures and flavours have been explored and enjoyed. Although many Indian dishes are fiery with chillies, there are others that are very mellow. Balti cuisine, which is Kashmiri cooking from the area that is now north Pakistan, is beautifully aromatic, but does not use chillies excessively, so it is not too hot. Many of the most familiar regional dishes we enjoy come from northern India, for example the mild kormas. The most fiery spice blends, however, come from southern India, including an abundance of vegetarian dishes using lentils, beans and chickpeas. Fragrant jasmine rice is another speciality of southern India. Coconuts are favourite ingredients of eastern India, and are used for making both sweet and savoury dishes, including deliciously creamy sauces. From western India there are recipes using dairy products, including yogurt and buttermilk, and the dishes are also accompanied by all kinds of unusual pickles.

All of these fabulous types of dish are brought together here in this collection of 180 vegetarian recipes, with their creative and adventurous combinations of vegetables, nuts, beans, peas, rice, lentils, fruit, herbs, spices and flavourings. The book offers all the vegetarian classics the home chef could ask for, including soups and appetizers, main dishes, rice and lentil dishes, side dishes, salads, relishes and chutneys, as well as breads, desserts and drinks – in fact everything you need to create the perfect vegetarian meal, whether it be a small evening supper or a lavish dinner party for friends and family.

The book includes a wide range of Indian recipes, such as Curried Carrot and Apple Soup, Vegetable Kashmiri, Spinach Dhal, Vegetable Samosas, Aubergine and Sweet Potato Stew with Coconut Milk, Karahi Shredded Cabbage with Mangetouts and Corn, Sweet-and-sour Raita, Spiced Naan, Onion, Mango and Peanut Chaat, Baked Rice Pudding, Sugar Bread Rolls, and Caramel Custard with Fresh Fruit.

Many recipes are quick to prepare with the simplest of combinations, whereas others call for a more varied store of spices and flavourings, including some lesser-known ingredients, such as mango powder (amchur) and compressed tamarind. Most of these special ingredients are available from supermarkets and markets, and sometimes even health-food stores. It's well worth visiting a specialist store or market if you have one nearby – large bags of whole spices are often sold cheaply, and these are ideal if you enjoy preparing spicy food regularly.

For the best flavour, always grind your spices just before you use them. You will immediately notice the strength of their aroma compared to spices that are bought ready ground. However, most of us want to take advantage of making quick spicy meals without a fuss and long periods of preparation, so ground spices might therefore be the best bet for busy people. Always buy ground spices in small quantities from a reputable supplier who has a quick turnover of stock, because once a spice has been ground it begins to lose its aroma and flavour. Don't be tempted to buy large quantities of ground spices, as you will lose out on taste.

To add an authentic touch to your vegetarian Indian meal, try cooking and serving it in a karahi. This piece of specialist equipment is a little like a wok but is more rounded in shape and is made of heavier metal. Traditionally, the karahi is made of cast iron, although a variety of metals are now used. Karahis are available in various sizes, including small ones for cooking single portions. Before you buy a karahi, however, it is important to check whether you can use it on your particular type of stove. You can use a wok or large frying pan in place of a karahi for cooking most types of Indian dish. Another piece of equipment that is useful for cooking Indian meals is a heat diffuser. This is placed between the pan and the heat source, its function being to reduce the heat so that curries can simmer at the lowest possible temperature.

Once you have sourced your ingredients and chosen your cooking vessel, you are ready to create any of the tantalizing vegetarian dishes contained in this book; your family and friends are in for a gastronomic treat.

Tomato & Coriander Soup

Although soups are not often eaten in India or Pakistan, tomato soup bucks the trend and is very popular. This is excellent on a cold winter's day.

Serves 4

675g/1½lb tomatoes, peeled and chopped
15ml/1 tbsp oil
1 bay leaf
4 spring onions (scallions), chopped
5ml/1 tsp salt
2.5ml/½ tsp crushed garlic
5ml/1 tsp crushed black peppercorns
30ml/2 tbsp chopped fresh coriander (cilantro)
750ml/1¼ pints/3 cups water
15ml/1 tbsp cornflour (cornstarch)
30ml/2 tbsp single (light) cream, to garnish (optional)

1 To peel the tomatoes, plunge them in very hot water, leave for 30 seconds, then take them out. The skin should now peel off easily. If not, put the tomatoes back in the water for a little longer. Once they have been peeled, roughly chop the tomatoes.

2 In a medium, heavy pan, heat the oil and fry the tomatoes, bay leaf and spring onions for a few minutes until soft.

3 Gradually add the salt, garlic, peppercorns and coriander. Pour in the water. Stir, then simmer gently over a low heat for 15–20 minutes.

4 Meanwhile, dissolve the cornflour in a little cold water to form a thick creamy paste.

5 Remove the soup from the heat and leave to cool slightly for a few minutes. Press through a sieve (strainer), or purée in a blender or food processor.

6 Return the puréed soup to the pan, add the cornflour mixture and stir over a gentle heat for about 3 minutes until thickened.

7 Pour the soup into individual serving dishes and garnish with a swirl of cream, if using. Serve hot.

Energy 76kcal/315kJ; Fat 3.4g; Saturated fat 0.43g; Carbohydrate 10.1g; Fibre 1.9g.

Curried Carrot & Apple Soup

The combination of carrot, curry powder and apple is a highly successful one. Curried fruit is delicious.

Serves 4

10ml/2 tsp sunflower oil
15ml/1 tbsp mild korma curry powder
500g/1¼lb carrots, chopped
1 large onion, chopped
1 tart cooking apple, chopped
750ml/1¼ pints/3 cups vegetable stock
salt and ground black pepper
plain yogurt and carrot curls, to garnish

1 Heat the oil in a large, heavy pan. Add the curry powder and fry for 2–3 minutes.

2 Add the carrots, onion and cooking apple and stir well until coated with the curry powder. Cover the pan.

3 Cook over low heat for about 15 minutes, shaking the pan occasionally, until soft. Spoon the vegetable mixture into a food processor or blender, then add half the stock and process until the mixture is smooth.

4 Return to the pan and pour in the remaining stock. Bring the soup to the boil and adjust the seasoning before serving in bowls, garnished with a swirl of yogurt and a few curls of raw carrot.

Variations
• Parsnips also taste great in a curried soup. Simply replace the carrots with chopped parsnips, or, if you prefer, use half the amount of carrots and half of parsnips.
• If you don't have any korma powder you can make up your own with 5ml/1 tsp each ground turmeric, cumin, coriander and cinnamon. Add 10ml/2 tsp grated fresh root ginger if you want to give your soup a little more kick.

Energy 89kcal/371kJ; Fat 2g; Saturated fat 0.3g; Carbohydrate 17.2g; Fibre 4.3g.

Fiery Hot Yogurt & Chilli Soup

Hot chillies, cool yogurt –
this is an unusual and tasty
soup with a real punch.

Serves 2–3
450ml/³⁄₄ pint/scant 2 cups
   natural (plain) low-fat yogurt,
   beaten
60ml/4 tbsp gram flour
2.5ml/½ tsp chilli powder
2.5ml/½ tsp ground turmeric
2 fresh green chillies, finely
   chopped
30ml/2 tbsp vegetable oil
4 whole dried red chillies
5ml/1 tsp cumin seeds
3 or 4 curry leaves
3 garlic cloves, crushed
5cm/2in piece fresh root
   ginger, crushed
salt
fresh coriander (cilantro) leaves,
   chopped, to garnish

1 Mix the yogurt, gram flour, chilli powder, turmeric and salt
to taste in a bowl. Press the mixture through a strainer into
a pan. Add the green chillies and simmer for 10 minutes,
stirring occasionally.

2 Heat the vegetable oil in a heavy pan and fry the remaining
spices, crushed garlic and fresh ginger until the dried chillies
turn black.

3 Pour the oil and the spices over the yogurt soup, cover the
pan and leave to rest for 5 minutes off the heat. Mix well and
gently reheat for a further 5 minutes. Ladle into warmed soup
bowls and serve hot, garnished with the coriander leaves.

> **Cook's Tips**
> • *For a lower-fat version drain off some of the oil before adding
> it to the yogurt. Low-fat yogurt makes this a healthy soup.*
> • *Adjust the amount of chilli according to how hot you want
> the soup to be.*

Spiced Cauliflower Soup

Light and tasty, this creamy,
mildly spicy vegetable soup
is multi-purpose. It makes a
wonderful warming first
course, an appetizing quick
meal and is delicious chilled.

Serves 4–6
1 large potato, diced
1 small cauliflower, chopped
1 onion, chopped
15ml/1 tbsp oil
1 garlic clove, crushed
15ml/1 tbsp grated fresh
   root ginger
10ml/2 tsp ground turmeric
5ml/1 tsp cumin seeds
5ml/1 tsp black mustard seeds
10ml/2 tsp ground coriander
1 litre/1³⁄₄ pints/4 cups vegetable
   stock
300ml/½ pint/1¼ cups natural
   (plain) low-fat yogurt
salt and ground black pepper
fresh coriander (cilantro) or
   parsley, to garnish

1 Put the potato, cauliflower and onion into a large, heavy pan
with the oil and 45ml/3 tbsp water. Heat until hot and bubbling,
then stir well, cover the pan and turn the heat down. Continue
cooking the mixture for about 10 minutes.

2 Add the garlic, ginger and spices. Stir well, and cook for
another 2 minutes, stirring occasionally. Pour in the stock and
season well. Bring to the boil, then cover and simmer for about
20 minutes. Purée in a food processor and return to the pan.
Stir in the yogurt, adjust the seasoning, and serve garnished with
coriander or parsley.

> **Cook's Tip**
> *A freshly made stock always tastes best. To make home-made
> vegetable stock, add to 3.5 litres/6 pints/15 cups of water:
> 2 sliced leeks, 3 chopped celery sticks, 1 chopped onion,
> 1 chopped parsnip, 1 seeded and chopped yellow (bell)
> pepper, 3 crushed garlic cloves, fresh herbs and 45ml/3 tbsp
> light soy sauce. Season, then slowly bring to the boil. Lower the
> heat and simmer for 30 minutes, stirring from time to time.
> Leave to cool. Strain, discard the vegetables, and use the stock
> as indicated in the recipe.*

Energy 188kcal/789kJ; Fat 5.4g; Saturated fat 0.77g; Carbohydrate 24.6g; Fibre 3g.

Energy 321kcal/1344kJ; Fat 13.7g; Saturated fat 2.5g; Carbohydrate 33.8g; Fibre 1.5g.

Onion Bhajias

A favourite snack in India, bhajias consist of a savoury vegetable mixture in a crisp and spicy batter. They can be served as an appetizer or as a side dish with curries.

Makes 20–25
2 large onions
225g/8oz/2 cups gram flour
2.5ml/½ tsp chilli powder
5ml/1 tsp ground turmeric
5ml/1 tsp baking powder
1.5ml/¼ tsp asafoetida

2.5ml/½ tsp each nigella, fennel, cumin and onion seeds, coarsely crushed
2 fresh green chillies, finely chopped
50g/2oz/2 cups fresh coriander (cilantro), chopped
vegetable oil, for deep-frying
salt

1 Using a sharp knife, slice the onions into thin rounds. Separate the slices and set them aside on a plate.

2 In a bowl mix together the flour, chilli powder, ground turmeric, baking powder and asafoetida. Add salt to taste. Sift the mixture into a large mixing bowl.

3 Add the coarsely crushed seeds, onion slices, green chillies and fresh coriander and toss together well.

4 Add enough cold water to make a paste, then stir in more water to make a thick batter that coats the onions and spices.

5 Heat enough oil in a karahi or wok for deep-frying. Drop spoonfuls of the mixture into the hot oil and fry the bhajias until they are golden brown. Leave enough space to turn the bhajias. Drain well and serve hot.

Variation
This versatile batter can be used with other vegetables, including okra, cauliflower and broccoli.

Energy 157kcal/650kJ; Fat 12.7g; Saturated fat 1.5g; Carbohydrate 8.2g; Fibre 0.9g.

Vegetable Samosas

A selection of highly spiced vegetables in a pastry casing makes these samosas a delicious snack at any time of the day.

Makes 28
14 sheets of filo pastry, thawed and wrapped in a damp dish towel
oil, for brushing the pastries

For the filling
3 large potatoes, boiled and roughly mashed
75g/3oz/¾ cup frozen peas, thawed
50g/2oz/⅓ cup canned corn, drained

5ml/1 tsp ground coriander
5ml/1 tsp ground cumin
5ml/1 tsp dry mango powder (amchur)
1 small onion, finely chopped
2 fresh green chillies, finely chopped
30ml/2 tbsp coriander (cilantro) leaves, chopped
30ml/2 tbsp chopped fresh mint leaves
juice of 1 lemon
salt

1 Preheat the oven to 200°C/400°F/Gas 6. Cut each sheet of filo pastry in half lengthways and fold each piece in half lengthways to give 28 thin strips. Lightly brush with oil.

2 Toss all the filling ingredients together in a large mixing bowl until they are well blended. Adjust the seasoning with salt and lemon juice if necessary.

3 Using one strip of the pastry at a time, place 15ml/1 tbsp of the filling mixture at one end and fold the pastry diagonally over. Continue folding to form a triangle shape. Brush the samosas with oil. Bake for 10–15 minutes, until golden brown.

Cook's Tip
Work with one or two sheets of filo pastry at a time and keep the rest covered with a damp dish towel to prevent it drying out.

Energy 50kcal/205kJ; Fat 0.78g; Saturated fat 0.1g; Carbohydrate 9.4g; Fibre 0.5g.

Spiced Potato Cakes with Chickpeas

Fragrant and spicy chickpeas go very well with these fiery potato cakes.

Makes 10–12
30ml/2 tbsp vegetable oil
30ml/2 tbsp ground coriander
30ml/2 tbsp ground cumin
2.5ml/½ tsp ground turmeric
2.5ml/½ tsp salt
2.5ml/½ tsp granulated sugar
30ml/2 tbsp gram flour, mixed
    with a little water to make
    a paste
450g/1lb/3 cups cooked
    chickpeas, drained
2 fresh green chillies, chopped
5cm/2in piece fresh root ginger,
    crushed
75g/3oz/1½ cups fresh coriander
    (cilantro), chopped
2 firm tomatoes, chopped
fresh mint sprigs, to garnish

For the potato cakes
450g/1lb potatoes, boiled
    and mashed
4 fresh green chillies, finely
    chopped
50g/2oz/2 cups chopped fresh
    coriander
7.5ml/1½ tsp ground cumin
5ml/1 tsp dry mango powder
    (amchur)
vegetable oil, for frying
salt

1 Heat the oil in a karahi, wok or large pan. Add the coriander, cumin, turmeric, salt, sugar and gram flour paste and cook until the water has evaporated and the oil has separated.

2 Add the chickpeas to the spices in the pan, and stir in the chopped chillies, ginger, fresh coriander and tomatoes. Toss the ingredients well and simmer gently for about 5 minutes. Transfer to a serving dish and keep warm.

3 To make the potato cakes, place the mashed potato in a large bowl and add the green chillies, chopped fresh coriander, cumin, dry mango powder and salt. Mix together until all the ingredients are well blended.

4 Using your hands, shape the potato mixture into little cakes. Heat the oil in a shallow frying pan and fry the cakes on both sides until golden brown. Transfer to a serving dish, garnish with mint sprigs and serve with the spicy chickpeas.

Energy 91kcal/383kJ; Fat 3.3g; Saturated fat 0.4g; Carbohydrate 11.9g; Fibre 2.2g.

Spicy Toasts

These crunchy toasts make an ideal snack or part of a brunch. They are especially delicious served with grilled tomatoes.

Makes 4
4 eggs
300ml/½ pint/1¼ cups milk
2 fresh green chillies, finely
    chopped
30ml/2 tbsp chopped fresh
    coriander (cilantro)
75g/3oz/¾ cup grated Cheddar
    or mozzarella cheese
2.5ml/½ tsp salt
1.5ml/¼ tsp ground black
    pepper
4 slices bread
corn oil, for frying

1 Break the eggs into a medium bowl and whisk together. Slowly add the milk and whisk again. Add the chillies, coriander, cheese, salt and pepper, and mix well.

2 Cut the bread slices in half diagonally, and soak them, one at a time, in the egg mixture.

3 Heat the oil in a medium frying pan and fry the bread slices over a medium heat, turning them once or twice, until they are golden brown.

4 Drain off any excess oil as you remove the toasts from the pan, and serve immediately.

Variations
• You can also use these ingredients to make a spicy topping for toasted bread. Toast the sliced and halved bread on one side. Mix 115g/4oz cheese with the flavourings and spread on the untoasted side. Grill (broil) until bubbling and golden.
• Try garlic and wholegrain mustard in place of the chillies for toasting.
• Make it a creamy spread for toasting by adding 75g/3oz cubed and steamed butternut squash mashed with the cheese and flavourings.

Energy 267kcal/1118kJ; Fat 4.5g; Saturated fat 6.9g; Carbohydrate 17.8g; Fibre 0.9g

Aubergine Curry

A simple and delicious way of cooking aubergines which retains their full flavour.

Serves 4

2 large aubergines (eggplants)
115g/4oz/1½ cups button
  (white) mushrooms
15ml/1 tbsp oil
2.5ml/½ tsp black mustard seeds
1 bunch spring onions (scallions),
  finely chopped

2 garlic cloves, crushed
1 fresh red chilli, finely chopped
2.5ml/½ tsp chilli powder
5ml/1 tsp ground cumin
5ml/1 tsp ground coriander
1.5ml/¼ tsp ground turmeric
5ml/1 tsp salt
400g/14oz can chopped
  tomatoes
15ml/1 tbsp chopped fresh
  coriander (cilantro), plus a sprig
  to garnish

1 Preheat the oven to 200°C/400°F/Gas 6. Wrap each aubergine in foil and bake for 1 hour or until soft. Unwrap and leave to cool.

2 Cut the button mushrooms in half, or in quarters if large, and set aside.

3 While the aubergines are baking, heat the oil in a heavy pan and fry the mustard seeds for 2 minutes until they begin to splutter.

4 Add the spring onions, mushrooms, garlic and chilli and fry for 5 minutes. Stir in the chilli powder, cumin, ground coriander, turmeric and salt and fry for 3–4 minutes.

5 Add the tomatoes and simmer for 5 minutes.

6 Cut each of the cooked aubergines in half lengthways and scoop out the soft flesh into a mixing bowl. Mash the flesh roughly with a fork.

7 Add the mashed aubergines and chopped fresh coriander to the pan. Bring to the boil and simmer for 5 minutes or until the sauce thickens. Serve garnished with a fresh coriander sprig.

Stuffed Aubergines in Seasoned Tamarind Juice

This spicy aubergine dish will add a refreshing tang to any meal.

Serves 4

12 baby aubergines (eggplants)
30ml/2 tbsp vegetable oil
1 small onion, chopped
10ml/2 tsp grated fresh
  root ginger
10ml/2 tsp crushed garlic
5ml/1 tsp coriander seeds
5ml/1 tsp cumin seeds

10ml/2 tsp white poppy seeds
10ml/2 tsp sesame seeds
10ml/2 tsp desiccated (dry
  unsweetened shredded)
  coconut
15ml/1 tbsp dry-roasted skinned
  peanuts
2.5–5ml/½–1 tsp chilli powder
5ml/1 tsp salt
6–8 curry leaves
1 or 2 dried red chillies, chopped
2.5ml/½ tsp concentrated
  tamarind paste

1 Make three deep slits lengthways on each aubergine, without cutting through, then soak in salted water for 20 minutes. Drain and dry on kitchen paper.

2 Heat half the oil in a pan and sauté the onion for 3–4 minutes. Add the ginger and garlic and cook for 30 seconds. Add the coriander and cumin seeds and sauté for 30 seconds, then add the poppy seeds, sesame seeds and coconut. Sauté for 1 minute, stirring constantly. Leave to cool slightly, then grind the spices in a food processor, adding 105ml/7 tbsp warm water. The mixture should form a thick, slightly coarse paste.

3 Mix the peanuts, chilli powder and salt into the paste. Stuff the aubergine slits with the spice and reserve any remaining paste.

4 Heat the remaining oil in a karahi, wok or large pan over a medium heat and add the curry leaves and chillies. Let the chillies blacken, then add the aubergines and the tamarind blended with 105ml/7 tbsp hot water. Add any remaining spice paste and stir to mix. Cover the pan and simmer gently for 15–20 minutes or until the aubergines are tender. Serve with chapatis, if you like.

Energy 99kcal/413kJ; Fat 4.6g; Saturated fat 0.45g; Carbohydrate 10.4g; Fibre 6g.

Energy 141kcal/585kJ; Fat 12g; Saturated fat 1.7g; Carbohydrate 5.1g; Fibre 3.3g.

Aubergine & Sweet Potato Stew with Coconut Milk

Aubergines and sweet potatoes go well together and the coconut milk adds a mellow note.

Serves 6

400g/14oz baby aubergines (eggplants) or 2 standard aubergines

60ml/4 tbsp groundnut (peanut) oil

225g/8oz Thai red shallots or other small shallots or pickling onions

5ml/1 tsp fennel seeds, lightly crushed

4 or 5 garlic cloves, thinly sliced

25ml/1½ tbsp finely chopped fresh root ginger

475ml/16fl oz/2 cups vegetable stock

2 lemon grass stalks, outer layers discarded, finely chopped or minced (ground)

15g/½oz fresh coriander (cilantro), stalks and leaves chopped separately

3 kaffir lime leaves, lightly bruised

2 or 3 small fresh red chillies

45–60ml/3–4 tbsp Thai green curry paste

675g/1½lb sweet potatoes, peeled and cut into thick chunks

400ml/14fl oz/1⅔ cups coconut milk

2.5–5ml/½–1 tsp palm sugar or light muscovado (brown) sugar

250g/9oz/3½ cups mushrooms, thickly sliced

juice of 1 lime, to taste

salt and ground black pepper

boiled rice and 18 fresh Thai basil or ordinary basil leaves, to serve

1 Trim the aubergines. Slice baby aubergines in half lengthways. Cut standard aubergines into chunks.

2 Heat half the oil in a wide pan or deep, lidded frying pan. Add the aubergines and cook uncovered over medium heat, stirring occasionally, until lightly browned on all sides. Remove from the pan and set aside.

3 Slice 4 or 5 of the shallots. Cook the whole shallots in the oil remaining in the pan, adding a little more oil if necessary, until lightly browned. Set aside with the aubergines. Add the remaining oil to the pan and cook the sliced shallots, fennel seeds, garlic and ginger over a low heat for 5 minutes.

4 Pour in the vegetable stock, then add the lemon grass, chopped coriander stalks and any roots, lime leaves and whole chillies. Cover and simmer over a low heat for 5 minutes.

5 Stir in 30ml/2 tbsp of the curry paste and the sweet potatoes. Simmer gently for about 10 minutes, then return the aubergines and browned shallots to the pan and cook for a further 5 minutes.

6 Stir in the coconut milk and the sugar. Season to taste with salt and pepper, then stir in the mushrooms and simmer gently for 5 minutes, or until all the vegetables are cooked and tender. Stir in more curry paste and lime juice to taste, followed by the chopped coriander leaves. Adjust the seasoning, if necessary, and ladle the vegetables into warmed bowls. Sprinkle basil leaves over the stew and serve with rice.

Energy 225kcal/945kJ; Fat 10.3g; Saturated fat 1.4g; Carbohydrate 31.8g; Fibre 5.1g.

Curried Stuffed Peppers

Hot, spicy and delicious, these fabulous peppers are often prepared for weddings in Hyderabad.

Serves 4–6

15ml/1 tbsp sesame seeds

15ml/1 tbsp white poppy seeds

5ml/1 tsp coriander seeds

60ml/4 tbsp desiccated (dry unsweetened shredded) coconut

½ onion, sliced

2.5cm/1in piece fresh root ginger, sliced

4 garlic cloves, sliced

handful of fresh coriander (cilantro)

6 fresh green chillies

60ml/4 tbsp vegetable oil

2 potatoes, boiled and coarsely mashed

salt

2 each green, red and yellow (bell) peppers

30ml/2 tbsp sesame oil

5ml/1 tsp cumin seeds

60ml/4 tbsp tamarind juice

1 In a frying pan, dry-fry the sesame, poppy and coriander seeds, then add the coconut and continue to roast until the coconut turns golden brown. Add the onion, ginger, garlic, coriander, and 2 of the chillies, and roast for a further 5 minutes. Cool, and grind to a paste using a pestle and mortar or food processor. Set aside.

2 Heat 30ml/2 tbsp of the oil in a frying pan and fry the ground paste for 4–5 minutes. Add the potatoes and salt, and stir well until the spices have blended evenly into the potatoes.

3 Trim the bases of the peppers so that they stand, then slice off the tops and reserve. Remove the seeds and any white pith. Fill the peppers with equal amounts of the potato mixture and replace the tops.

4 Slit the remaining chillies and remove the seeds, if you like. Heat the sesame oil and remaining vegetable oil in a frying pan and fry the cumin seeds and the slit green chillies. When the chillies turn white, add the tamarind juice and bring to the boil. Place the peppers over the mixture, cover the pan and cook until the peppers are just tender. Serve immediately.

Energy 390kcal/1617kJ; Fat 27.3g; Saturated fat 10.4g; Carbohydrate 31.1g; Fibre 7.8g.

Balti Potatoes with Aubergines

Using baby potatoes adds to the attractiveness of this dish. Choose the smaller variety of aubergines, too, as they are tastier than the large ones, which contain a lot of water and little flavour. You can buy small aubergines from specialist grocers.

Serves 4

10–12 baby potatoes
6 small aubergines (eggplants)
1 medium red (bell) pepper
15ml/1 tbsp oil
2 medium onions, sliced

4–6 curry leaves
2.5ml/ ½ tsp onion seeds
5ml/1 tsp crushed coriander seeds
2.5ml/ ½ tsp cumin seeds
5ml/1 tsp grated fresh root ginger
5ml/1 tsp crushed garlic
5ml/1 tsp crushed dried red
 chillies
15ml/1 tbsp chopped fresh
 fenugreek leaves
5ml/1 tsp chopped fresh
 coriander (cilantro)
15ml/1 tbsp natural (plain)
 low-fat yogurt
fresh coriander leaves,
 to garnish

1 Cook the unpeeled potatoes in a pan of boiling water until they are just soft, but still whole.

2 Cut the aubergines into quarters if very small, or eighths if using larger aubergines.

3 Cut the pepper in half, remove the seeds and ribs, then slice the flesh into thin even strips.

4 Heat the oil in a karahi, wok or heavy pan and fry the sliced onions, curry leaves, onion seeds, crushed coriander seeds and cumin seeds until the onion slices are a soft golden brown, stirring constantly.

5 Add the ginger, garlic, crushed chillies and fenugreek, followed by the aubergines and potatoes. Stir everything together and cover the pan with a lid. Lower the heat and cook the vegetables for 5–7 minutes.

6 Remove the lid, add the fresh coriander followed by the yogurt and stir well. Serve garnished with coriander leaves.

Energy 183kcal/773kJ; Fat 4.42g; Saturated fat 0.70g; Carbohydrate 33.02g; Fibre 5.43g.

Balti Stir-fried Vegetables with Cashew Nuts

This quick and versatile stir-fry will accommodate most other combinations of vegetables – you do not have to use the selection suggested here.

Serves 4

2 medium carrots
1 medium red (bell) pepper,
 seeded
1 medium green (bell) pepper,
 seeded
2 courgettes (zucchini)

115g/4oz green beans
1 medium bunch spring onions
 (scallions)
15ml/1 tbsp oil
4–6 curry leaves
2.5ml/ ½ tsp cumin seeds
4 dried red chillies
10–12 cashew nuts
5ml/1 tsp salt
30ml/2 tbsp lemon juice
fresh mint leaves, to garnish

1 Prepare the vegetables: cut the carrots, peppers and courgettes into matchsticks, halve the beans and chop the spring onions. Set aside.

2 Heat the oil in a karahi, wok or heavy pan and fry the curry leaves, cumin seeds and dried red chillies for about 1 minute.

3 Add the vegetables and nuts, and stir them around gently. Add the salt and lemon juice. Continue to stir and cook for about 3–5 minutes.

4 Transfer the vegetables to a serving dish, garnish with fresh mint leaves and serve immediately.

Variation
Small florets of broccoli or cauliflower are delicious cooked in a stir-fry so that they retain their crunch. You could use them in place of the courgettes (zucchini). Or you could use mushrooms, mangetouts (snow peas) and beansprouts.

Energy 98kcal/406kJ; Fat 5.28g; Saturated fat 0.88g; Carbohydrate 10.36g; Fibre 3.94g.

Karahi Potatoes with Whole Spices

The potato is transformed into something quite exotic when it is cooked like this.

Serves 4
15ml/1 tbsp oil
5ml/1 tsp cumin seeds
3 curry leaves
5ml/1 tsp crushed dried red chillies
2.5ml/½ tsp mixed onion, mustard and fenugreek seeds
2.5ml/½ tsp fennel seeds
3 garlic cloves, sliced
2.5cm/1in piece fresh root ginger, grated
2 onions, sliced
6 new potatoes, thinly sliced
15ml/1 tbsp chopped fresh coriander (cilantro)
1 fresh red chilli, seeded and sliced
1 fresh green chilli, seeded and sliced

1 Heat the oil in a karahi, wok or heavy pan. Lower the heat slightly and add the cumin seeds, curry leaves, dried red chillies, mixed onion, mustard and fenugreek seeds, fennel seeds, garlic slices and ginger. Fry for 1 minute.

2 Add the onions and fry for a further 5 minutes, or until the onions are golden brown.

3 Add the potatoes, fresh coriander and sliced fresh red and green chillies and mix well. Cover the pan tightly with a lid or foil; if using foil, make sure that it does not touch the food. Cook over a very low heat for about 7 minutes or until the potatoes are tender.

4 Remove the pan from the heat, and take off the lid or foil cover. Serve hot straight from the pan.

Cook's Tip
Choose a waxy variety of new potato for this fairly hot vegetable dish; if you use a very soft potato, it will not be possible to cut it into thin slices without it breaking up. Suitable varieties are often labelled "salad potatoes" when sold at supermarkets. Leave the skin on for a tastier result.

Energy 110kcal/462kJ; Fat 3.6g; Saturated fat 0.39g; Carbohydrate 17.1g; Fibre 1.6g.

Balti Mushrooms in a Creamy Garlic Sauce

This is a simple and delicious Balti recipe which could be accompanied by bread or one of the rice dishes from this book.

Serves 4
350g/12oz/4½ cups button (white) mushrooms
15ml/1 tbsp oil
1 bay leaf
3 garlic cloves, roughly chopped
2 green chillies, seeded and chopped
225g/8oz/1 cup low-fat fromage frais or ricotta cheese
15ml/1 tbsp chopped fresh mint
15ml/1 tbsp chopped fresh coriander (cilantro)
5ml/1 tsp salt
fresh mint and coriander leaves, to garnish

1 Cut the button mushrooms in half, or in quarters if large, and set aside.

2 Heat the oil in a karahi, wok or heavy pan, then add the bay leaf, chopped garlic and chillies, and quickly stir-fry for about 1 minute.

3 Add the mushrooms. Stir-fry for another 2 minutes.

4 Remove from the heat and stir in the fromage frais or ricotta cheese, followed by the mint, coriander and salt. Return to the heat and stir-fry for 2–3 minutes, then transfer to a warmed serving dish and garnish with mint and coriander leaves.

Cook's Tip
Balti curries have their origins in Baltistan, the area that is now North Pakistan. They are traditionally aromatic but not heavily flavoured with chilli, and bread is usually used to scoop up the food. However, rice also goes well with all the dishes.

Energy 76kcal/321kJ; Fat 3.4g; Saturated fat 0.55g; Carbohydrate 5.2g; Fibre 1.1g.

Cauliflower & Coconut Milk Curry

A delicious vegetable stew which combines rich coconut milk with spices and is perfect as a vegetarian main course or as part of a buffet.

Serves 4
1 cauliflower
2 medium tomatoes
1 onion, chopped
2 garlic cloves, crushed
1 fresh green chilli, seeded
2.5ml/½ tsp ground turmeric
30ml/2 tbsp sunflower oil
400ml/14fl oz/1⅔ cups coconut milk
250ml/8fl oz/1 cup water
5ml/1 tsp granulated sugar
5ml/1 tsp tamarind pulp, soaked in 45ml/3 tbsp warm water
salt

1 Trim the stalk from the cauliflower and divide into tiny florets. Peel the tomatoes if you like, then chop them into 1–2.5cm/½–1in pieces.

2 Grind the chopped onion, garlic, green chilli and ground turmeric to a paste in a food processor.

3 Heat the oil in a karahi, wok or large frying pan and fry the spice paste to bring out the aromatic flavours, without allowing it to brown.

4 Add the cauliflower florets and toss well to coat in the spices. Stir in the coconut milk, water, sugar and salt to taste. Simmer for 5 minutes. Strain the tamarind and reserve the juice.

5 Add the tamarind juice and chopped tomatoes to the pan then cook for 2–3 minutes only. Taste and adjust the seasoning if necessary, then serve.

> **Cook's Tip**
> *Always be careful when preparing chillies as they can burn sensitive skin. Wear plastic gloves or wash hands thoroughly after preparation.*

Parsnip, Aubergine & Cashew Biryani

Full of the flavours of India, this hearty supper dish is great for chilly winter evenings.

Serves 4–6
1 small aubergine (eggplant), sliced
275g/10oz basmati rice
3 parsnips
3 onions
2 garlic cloves
2.5cm/1in piece fresh root ginger, peeled
about 60ml/4 tbsp vegetable oil
175g/6oz/1½ cups unsalted cashew nuts
40g/1½oz/3 tbsp sultanas (golden raisins)
1 red (bell) pepper, seeded and sliced
5ml/1 tsp ground cumin
5ml/1 tsp ground coriander
2.5ml/½ tsp chilli powder
120ml/4fl oz/½ cup natural (plain) yogurt
300ml/½ pint/1¼ cups vegetable stock
25g/1oz/2 tbsp butter
salt and ground black pepper
2 hard-boiled eggs, quartered, and sprigs of fresh coriander (cilantro), to garnish

1 Sprinkle the aubergine with salt and leave for 30 minutes. Rinse, pat dry and cut into bite-size pieces. Soak the rice in a bowl of cold water for 40 minutes. Peel and core the parsnips. Cut into 1cm/½in pieces. Process 1 onion, the garlic and ginger in a food processor. Add 30–45ml/2–3 tbsp water and process to a paste.

2 Finely slice the remaining onions. Heat 45ml/3 tbsp of the oil in a large flameproof casserole and fry the onions gently for 10–15 minutes until they are soft and deep golden brown. Remove and drain. Add 40g/1½oz of the cashew nuts to the pan and stir-fry for 2 minutes, checking that they do not burn. Add the sultanas and fry until they swell. Remove and drain on kitchen paper. Add the aubergine and pepper to the pan and stir-fry for 4–5 minutes. Drain on kitchen paper. Fry the parsnips for 4–5 minutes. Stir in the remaining cashew nuts and fry for 1 minute. Set aside.

3 Add the remaining 15ml/1 tbsp of oil to the pan. Add the onion paste. Cook, stirring, over moderate heat for 4–5 minutes, until the mixture turns golden. Stir in the cumin, coriander and chilli powder. Cook, stirring, for 1 minute, then reduce the heat and add the yogurt.

4 Bring the mixture slowly to the boil and stir in the stock, parsnips, aubergine and peppers. Season with salt and pepper, cover and simmer for 30–40 minutes, until the parsnips are tender, and then transfer to an ovenproof casserole.

5 Preheat the oven to 150°C/300°F/Gas 2. Drain the rice and add to 300ml/½ pint/1¼ cups salted boiling water. Cook gently for 5–6 minutes, until the rice is tender but slightly undercooked.

6 Drain the rice and pile it in a mound on top of the parsnips. Make a hole from the top to the base using the handle of a wooden spoon. Sprinkle the reserved fried onions, cashew nuts and sultanas over the rice and dot with butter. Cover with a double layer of foil, then secure in place with a lid. Cook in the oven for 35–40 minutes. Serve garnished with eggs and coriander.

Energy 119kcal/495kJ; Fat 6.7g; Saturated fat 1.1g; Carbohydrate 11.5g; Fibre 2.3g.

Energy 824kcal/3430kJ; Fat 40.7g; Saturated fat 9.4g; Carbohydrate 96.4g; Fibre 9.1g.

Mushroom Curry

This is a delicious way of cooking mushrooms. It goes well with other dishes, but is also great served on its own.

Serves 4
30ml/2 tbsp oil
2.5ml/½ tsp cumin seeds
1.5ml/¼ tsp black peppercorns
4 green cardamom pods
1.5ml/¼ tsp ground turmeric
1 onion, finely chopped
5ml/1 tsp ground cumin

5ml/1 tsp ground coriander
2.5ml/½ tsp garam masala
1 fresh green chilli, finely chopped
2 garlic cloves, crushed
2.5cm/1in piece fresh root ginger, grated
400g/14oz can chopped tomatoes
1.5ml/¼ tsp salt
450g/1lb/6 cups button (white) mushrooms, halved
chopped fresh coriander (cilantro), to garnish

1 Heat the oil in a large, heavy pan and fry the cumin seeds, peppercorns, cardamom pods and turmeric for 2–3 minutes.

2 Add the onion and fry for about 5 minutes until golden. Stir in the cumin, ground coriander and garam masala and fry for a further 2 minutes.

3 Add the chilli, garlic and ginger and fry for 2–3 minutes, stirring all the time to prevent the spices from sticking to the pan. Add the tomatoes and salt. Bring to the boil and simmer for 5 minutes.

4 Add the mushrooms. Cover and simmer over a low heat for 10 minutes. Garnish with chopped coriander before serving.

> **Cook's Tip**
> *The distinctive flavour of mushrooms goes well with this mixture of spices. If you don't want to use button (white) mushrooms, you can substitute any other mushrooms. Dried mushrooms can be added, if you like. Their intense flavour holds its own against the taste of the curry spices. Soak dried mushrooms before using, and add them to the recipe with the tomatoes.*

Energy 113kcal/469kJ; Fat 6.9g; Saturated fat 0.88g; Carbohydrate 8.8g; Fibre 2.5g.

Mushrooms with Garlic & Chilli Sauce

When you are planning a barbecue for friends and family, it can be tricky finding something really special for the vegetarians in the party. These tasty mushroom kebabs are ideal because they look, smell and taste absolutely wonderful.

Serves 4
12 large field (portabello), chestnut or oyster mushrooms or a mixture, cut in half
4 garlic cloves, coarsely chopped

6 coriander (cilantro) roots, coarsely chopped
15ml/1 tbsp granulated sugar
30ml/2 tbsp light soy sauce
ground black pepper

For the dipping sauce
15ml/1 tbsp granulated sugar
90ml/6 tbsp rice vinegar
5ml/1 tsp salt
1 garlic clove, crushed
1 small fresh red chilli, seeded and finely chopped

1 If using wooden skewers, soak them in cold water for at least 30 minutes to prevent them burning over the barbecue or under the grill (broiler). You will need eight skewers.

2 Make the dipping sauce by heating the sugar, rice vinegar and salt in a small pan, stirring occasionally until the sugar and salt have dissolved. Add the garlic and chilli, pour into a serving dish and keep warm.

3 Thread three mushroom halves on to each skewer. Lay the filled skewers side by side in a shallow dish.

4 In a mortar or spice grinder pound or blend the garlic and coriander roots. Scrape into a bowl and mix with the sugar, soy sauce and a little pepper.

5 Brush the soy sauce mixture over the mushrooms and leave to marinate for 15 minutes. Prepare the barbecue or preheat the grill (broiler) and cook the mushrooms for 2–3 minutes on each side. Serve with the dipping sauce.

Energy 55kcal/231kJ; Fat 1.3g; Saturated fat 0.3g; Carbohydrate 6.2g; Fibre 3.1g.

Mushroom & Okra Curry

The sliced okra not only flavours this unusual curry, but thickens it, too.

Serves 4

4 garlic cloves, roughly chopped
2.5cm/1in piece fresh root ginger, roughly chopped
1 or 2 fresh red chillies, seeded and chopped
175ml/6fl oz/³⁄₄ cup cold water
15ml/1 tbsp sunflower oil
5ml/1 tsp coriander seeds
5ml/1 tsp cumin seeds
5ml/1 tsp ground cumin
seeds from 2 green cardamom pods, ground
pinch of ground turmeric
400g/14oz can chopped tomatoes
450g/1lb/6 cups mushrooms, quartered if large
225g/8oz okra, trimmed and sliced
30ml/2 tbsp chopped fresh coriander (cilantro)
basmati rice, to serve

For the mango relish

1 large ripe mango, about 500g/1¼lb
1 small garlic clove, crushed
1 small onion, finely chopped
10ml/2 tsp grated fresh root ginger
1 fresh red chilli, seeded and finely chopped
a pinch each of salt and sugar

1 To make the mango relish, peel the mango, cut the flesh off the stone and chop it finely. Put it in a bowl. Mash with a fork and mix in the garlic, onion, ginger, chilli, salt and sugar. Set aside.

2 Put the garlic, ginger, chillies and 45ml/3 tbsp of the water in a blender or food processor and blend to a smooth paste.

3 Heat the oil in a large pan. Add the coriander and cumin seeds, and the ground cumin, ground cardamom and turmeric, and cook for 1 minute, until aromatic. Scrape in the garlic paste, then add the tomatoes, mushrooms and okra. Pour in the remaining water. Stir to mix well, and bring to the boil. Reduce the heat, cover and simmer the curry for 5 minutes.

4 Remove the lid, increase the heat slightly and cook for 5–10 minutes more, until the okra is tender. Stir in the fresh coriander and serve with the rice and the mango relish.

Mushrooms, Peas & Paneer

Paneer is a traditional cheese made from rich milk and is most popular with northern Indians. Rajasthani farmers eat this dish for lunch with thick parathas as they work in the fields.

Serves 4–6

75ml/6 tbsp ghee or vegetable oil
225g/8oz paneer, cubed
1 onion, finely chopped
a few fresh mint leaves, chopped
50g/2oz/2 cups fresh coriander (cilantro), chopped
3 fresh green chillies, chopped
3 garlic cloves, roughly chopped
2.5cm/1in piece fresh root ginger, sliced
5ml/1 tsp ground turmeric
5ml/1 tsp chilli powder (optional)
5ml/1 tsp garam masala
salt
225g/8oz/3 cups tiny button (white) mushrooms
225g/8oz/2 cups frozen peas, thawed and drained
175ml/6fl oz/³⁄₄ cup natural (plain) yogurt, mixed with 5ml/1 tsp cornflour (cornstarch)
fresh mint sprig, to garnish

1 Heat the ghee or vegetable oil in a frying pan and fry the paneer cubes until they are golden brown on all sides. Remove and drain on kitchen paper.

2 Grind the onion, mint, coriander, chillies, garlic and ginger in a pestle and mortar or food processor to a fairly smooth paste. Remove and mix in the turmeric, chilli powder if using, garam masala and salt.

3 Remove the excess ghee or oil from the pan, leaving about 15ml/1 tbsp. Heat and fry the paste until the raw onion smell disappears and the oil separates.

4 Add the mushrooms, peas and paneer. Mix together well. Cool the mixture and gradually fold in the yogurt. Simmer for about 10 minutes. Garnish with a sprig of mint and serve hot.

Energy 152kcal/645kJ; Fat 4.4g; Saturated fat 0.7g; Carbohydrate 24.2g; Fibre 8g.

Energy 294kcal/1217kJ; Fat 20.3g; Saturated fat 3.7g; Carbohydrate 14g; Fibre 3.5g.

Okra with Green Mango & Lentils

If you like okra, you'll love this spicy tangy dish. Serve with rice for a main course.

Serves 4

115g/4oz/½ cup toor dhal or
   yellow split peas
450g/1lb okra
15ml/1 tbsp oil
2.5ml/½ tsp onion seeds
2 onions, sliced
2.5ml/½ tsp ground fenugreek

1.5ml/¼ tsp ground turmeric
5ml/1 tsp ground coriander
7.5ml/1½ tsp chilli powder
5ml/1 tsp grated fresh
   root ginger
5ml/1 tsp crushed garlic
1 green mango, peeled and sliced
7.5ml/1½ tsp salt
2 red chillies, seeded and sliced
30ml/2 tbsp chopped fresh
   coriander (cilantro)
1 tomato, sliced

1 Wash the toor dhal thoroughly to remove any grit and place in a large pan with enough cold water to cover. Bring to the boil and cook for 30–45 minutes until soft but not mushy.

2 Trim the okra and cut the pods into 1cm/½in pieces.

3 Heat the oil in a karahi, wok or heavy pan and fry the onion seeds until they begin to pop. Add the onions and fry until golden brown. Lower the heat and stir in the ground fenugreek, turmeric and coriander, and the chilli powder, ginger and garlic.

4 Add the mango slices and the okra pieces. Stir well and then add the salt, red chillies and fresh coriander. Stir-fry together for 3–4 minutes or until the okra is well cooked and tender.

5 Finally, add the cooked dhal and sliced tomato, and cook for a further 3 minutes. Serve hot.

Cook's Tip
When buying okra, always choose small, bright-green ones with no brown patches. If cooking whole, trim off the conical cap, taking care not to pierce through to the seed pod where there are tiny edible seeds and a sticky juice.

Energy 229kcal/963kJ; Fat 5g; Saturated fat 0.55g; Carbohydrate 36g; Fibre 8.1g.

Corn & Pea Curry

Tender corn cooked in a spicy tomato sauce makes a flavoursome curry. It is perfect served with chapatis.

Serves 4

6 frozen corn cobs, thawed
15ml/1 tbsp oil
2.5ml/½ tsp cumin seeds
1 onion, finely chopped
2 garlic cloves, crushed
1 fresh green chilli, finely chopped
15ml/1 tbsp curry paste
5ml/1 tsp ground coriander
5ml/1 tsp ground cumin
1.5ml/¼ tsp ground turmeric

2.5ml/½ tsp salt
2.5ml/½ tsp granulated
   sugar
400g/14oz can chopped
   tomatoes
15ml/1 tbsp tomato purée
   (paste)
150ml/¼ pint/⅔ cup
   water
115g/4oz/1 cup frozen peas,
   thawed
30ml/2 tbsp chopped fresh
   coriander (cilantro)
chapatis, to serve (optional)

1 Using a sharp knife, cut each piece of corn in half crossways to make 12 equal pieces in total.

2 Bring a large pan of water to the boil and cook the corn cob pieces for 10–12 minutes. Drain well.

3 Heat the oil in a large, heavy pan and fry the cumin seeds for 2 minutes or until they begin to splutter. Add the onion, garlic and chilli and fry for about 5–6 minutes until the onion is golden.

4 Add the curry paste and fry for 2 minutes. Stir in the remaining spices, the salt and sugar, and fry for a further 2–3 minutes, adding some water if the mixture is too dry.

5 Add the chopped tomatoes and tomato purée together with the water and simmer for 5 minutes or until the sauce thickens. Add the peas and cook for a further 5 minutes.

6 Stir in the pieces of corn and the fresh coriander and cook for 6–8 minutes more, until the corn and peas are tender. Serve with chapatis for mopping up the rich sauce, if you like.

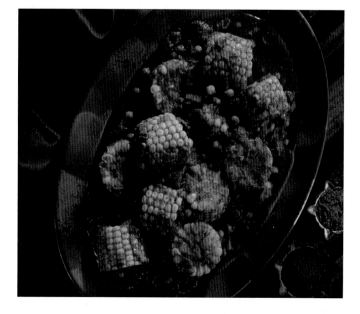

Energy 159kcal/669kJ; Fat 5.2g; Saturated fat 0.48g; Carbohydrate 23g; Fibre 4.6g.

Spinach & Potato Curry

Spinach, potatoes and traditional Indian spices are the main ingredients in this simple but authentic curry.

Serves 4

450g/1lb spinach
15ml/1 tbsp oil
5ml/1 tsp black mustard seeds
1 onion, thinly sliced
2 garlic cloves, crushed
2.5cm/1in piece fresh root ginger, finely chopped
675g/1½lb potatoes, cut into 2.5cm/1in chunks
5ml/1 tsp chilli powder
5ml/1 tsp salt
120ml/4fl oz/½ cup water

1 Wash and trim the spinach, then blanch it in a pan of boiling water for about 3–4 minutes.

2 Drain the spinach thoroughly and set aside. When it is cool enough to handle, use your hands to squeeze out any remaining liquid (see Cook's Tip) and set aside.

3 Heat the oil in a large, heavy pan and fry the mustard seeds for 2 minutes or until they splutter.

4 Add the sliced onion, garlic cloves and chopped ginger to the mustard seeds and fry for 5 minutes, stirring.

5 Add the potato chunks, chilli powder, salt and water, and cook for a further 8 minutes.

6 Add the drained spinach. Cover the pan with a lid and simmer for 10–15 minutes or until the potatoes are tender. Serve hot.

Cook's Tips
• To make certain that the spinach is completely dry, put it in a clean dish towel, roll up tightly and squeeze gently to remove any excess liquid.
• Use a waxy variety of potato for this dish so that the pieces do not break up during cooking.

Spicy Potato & Tomato Curry

Diced potatoes are cooked gently in a fresh tomato sauce, which is flavoured with curry leaves, green chillies and ginger.

Serves 4

2 medium potatoes
15ml/1 tbsp oil
2 medium onions, finely chopped
4 curry leaves
1.5ml/¼ tsp onion seeds
1 fresh green chilli, seeded and chopped
4 tomatoes, sliced
5ml/1 tsp grated fresh root ginger
5ml/1 tsp crushed garlic
5ml/1 tsp chilli powder
5ml/1 tsp ground coriander
1.5ml/¼ tsp salt
5ml/1 tsp lemon juice
15ml/1 tbsp chopped fresh coriander (cilantro)
3 hard-boiled eggs, to garnish

1 Peel the potatoes and cut them into small cubes.

2 Heat the oil in a karahi, wok or heavy pan and stir-fry the onions, curry leaves, onion seeds and green chilli for about 40 seconds.

3 Add the tomatoes and cook for about 2 minutes over a low heat.

4 Add the ginger and garlic, chilli powder, ground coriander and salt to taste. Continue to stir-fry for 1–2 minutes, then add the potatoes and cook over a low heat for 5–7 minutes until the potatoes are tender.

5 Add the lemon juice and fresh coriander and stir to mix together.

6 Shell the hard-boiled eggs, cut into quarters, and add as a garnish to the finished dish.

Cook's Tip
Use vine-ripened tomatoes, if possible, for the best flavour. Locally grown tomatoes in season are also more likely to have a full flavour than those bought out of season.

Energy 203kcal/851kJ; Fat 4.6g; Saturated fat 0.65g; Carbohydrate 34.4g; Fibre 5.1g.

Energy 188kcal/790kJ; Fat 7.62g; Saturated fat 1.66g; Carbohydrate 23.41g; Fibre 3.1g.

Courgette Curry with Tomatoes

Thickly sliced courgettes are combined with authentic Indian spices for a tasty vegetable curry.

Serves 4

675g/1½lb courgettes (zucchini)
30ml/2 tbsp oil
2.5ml/½ tsp cumin seeds
2.5ml/½ tsp mustard seeds
1 onion, thinly sliced
2 garlic cloves, crushed
1.5ml/¼ tsp ground turmeric
1.5ml/¼ tsp chilli powder
5ml/1 tsp ground coriander
5ml/1 tsp ground cumin
2.5ml/½ tsp salt
15ml/1 tbsp tomato purée (paste)
400g/14oz can chopped tomatoes
150ml/¼ pint/⅔ cup water
15ml/1 tbsp chopped fresh coriander (cilantro)
5ml/1 tsp garam masala
rice or naan bread, to serve

1 Trim the ends from the courgettes and then cut them evenly into 1cm/½in thick slices.

2 Heat the oil in a large, heavy pan and fry the cumin and the mustard seeds for 2 minutes until they begin to splutter.

3 Add the sliced onion and crushed garlic to the seeds in the pan, and fry for about 5–6 minutes.

4 Add the turmeric, chilli powder, ground coriander, cumin and salt, and fry for 2–3 minutes.

5 Add the sliced courgettes all at once, and cook for 5 minutes, stirring so that they do not burn.

6 Mix together the tomato purée and chopped tomatoes and add to the pan with the water. Cover and simmer for 10 minutes until the sauce thickens.

7 Stir in the fresh coriander and garam masala, then cook for 5 minutes or until the courgettes are tender. Serve the curry with rice or naan bread.

Potatoes Stuffed with Cottage Cheese

This makes an excellent low-fat meal at any time of the day.

Serves 4

4 medium baking potatoes
225g/8oz/1 cup low-fat cottage cheese
10ml/2 tsp tomato purée (paste)
2.5ml/½ tsp ground cumin
2.5ml/½ tsp ground coriander
2.5ml/½ tsp chilli powder
2.5ml/½ tsp salt
15ml/1 tbsp oil
2.5ml/½ tsp mixed onion and mustard seeds
3 curry leaves
30ml/2 tbsp water

For the garnish

mixed salad leaves
fresh coriander (cilantro) sprigs
lemon wedges
2 tomatoes, quartered

1 Preheat the oven to 180°C/350°F/Gas 4. Wash each potato and pat dry. Make a slit in the middle of each potato. Prick the potatoes a few times with a fork or skewer, then wrap them individually in foil. Bake in the oven directly on the shelf for about 1 hour, or until soft. Put the cottage cheese into a heatproof dish and set aside.

2 In a separate bowl, mix the tomato purée, ground cumin, ground coriander, chilli powder and salt.

3 Heat the oil in a small pan for about 1 minute. Add the mixed onion and mustard seeds and the curry leaves. When the curry leaves turn a shade darker, pour the tomato purée mixture into the pan and turn the heat immediately to low. Add the water and mix well. Cook for a further minute, then pour the spicy tomato mixture on to the cottage cheese and stir together well.

4 Check that the baked potatoes are cooked right through, by inserting a knife or skewer into the middle of the flesh. If it is soft, unwrap the potatoes from the foil and divide the cottage cheese equally between them.

5 Garnish the filled potatoes with mixed salad leaves, coriander sprigs, lemon wedges and tomato quarters and serve hot.

Energy 133kcal/550kJ; Fat 7.2g; Saturated fat 0.91g; Carbohydrate 11.6g; Fibre 2.8g.

Energy 175kcal/740kJ; Fat 4.3g; Saturated fat 0.43g; Carbohydrate 24.4g; Fibre 1.9g.

Spicy Root Vegetable Gratin

Subtly spiced, this rich gratin is substantial enough to serve on its own for lunch or supper.

Serves 4

2 large potatoes, total weight
   about 450g/1lb
2 sweet potatoes, total weight
   about 275g/10oz
175g/6oz celeriac
15ml/1 tbsp unsalted (sweet)
   butter
5ml/1 tsp curry powder
5ml/1 tsp ground turmeric
2.5ml/½ tsp ground coriander
5ml/1 tsp mild chilli powder
3 shallots, chopped
150ml/¼ pint/⅔ cup single
   (light) cream
150ml/¼ pint/⅔ cup milk
salt and ground black pepper
chopped fresh flat leaf parsley,
   to garnish

1 Peel the potatoes, sweet potatoes and celeriac and cut into thin, even slices using a sharp knife or the slicing attachment on a food processor. Immediately place the vegetables in a bowl of cold water to prevent them from discolouring.

2 Preheat the oven to 180°C/350°F/Gas 4. Heat half the butter in a heavy pan, add the curry powder, ground turmeric and coriander and half the chilli powder. Cook for 2 minutes, then leave to cool slightly. Drain the vegetables, then pat them dry with kitchen paper. Place in a bowl, add the spice mixture and the shallots, and mix well.

3 Arrange the vegetables in a shallow baking dish, seasoning well with salt and pepper between the layers. Mix the cream and milk together, pour the mixture over the vegetables, then sprinkle the remaining chilli powder on top.

4 Cover the dish with baking parchment and bake for 45 minutes. Remove the baking parchment, dot the vegetables with the remaining butter and bake for a further 50 minutes, or until the top is golden brown. Serve the gratin garnished with chopped parsley.

Energy 205kcal/863kJ; Fat 5.1g; Saturated fat 2.9g; Carbohydrate 36.9g; Fibre 4.7g.

Stuffed Baby Vegetables

The combination of potatoes and aubergines is popular in Indian cooking.

Serves 4

12 small potatoes
8 baby aubergines (eggplants)

For the stuffing
15ml/1 tbsp sesame seeds
30ml/2 tbsp ground coriander
30ml/2 tbsp ground cumin
2.5ml/½ tsp salt
1.5ml/¼ tsp chilli powder
2.5ml/½ tsp ground turmeric
10ml/2 tsp granulated sugar
1.5ml/¼ tsp garam masala
15ml/1 tbsp gram flour
2 garlic cloves, crushed
15ml/1 tbsp lemon juice
30ml/2 tbsp chopped fresh
   coriander (cilantro)

For the sauce
15ml/1 tbsp oil
2.5ml/½ tsp black mustard
   seeds
400g/14oz can chopped
   tomatoes
30ml/2 tbsp chopped fresh
   coriander
150ml/¼ pint/⅔ cup water

1 Preheat the oven to 200°C/400°F/Gas 6. Make deep slits in the potatoes and aubergines to hold the stuffing, ensuring that you do not cut right through.

2 Mix all the ingredients for the stuffing together on a plate.

3 Carefully spoon the spicy stuffing mixture into each of the slits in the potatoes and aubergines.

4 Arrange the stuffed potatoes and aubergines in a greased ovenproof dish, filling side up.

5 For the sauce, heat the oil in a heavy pan and fry the mustard seeds for 2 minutes until they begin to splutter, then add the canned tomatoes, chopped coriander and any leftover stuffing. Stir in the water. Bring to the boil and simmer for 5 minutes until the sauce thickens.

6 Pour the sauce over the potatoes and aubergines. Cover and bake in the oven for 25–30 minutes until the potatoes and aubergines are soft.

Energy 259kcal/1088kJ; Fat 7.6g; Saturated fat 0.73g; Carbohydrate 41.3g; Fibre 4g.

Mixed Vegetable Curry

You can use any combination of vegetables that are in season for this basic recipe.

Serves 4
15ml/1 tbsp oil
2.5ml/½ tsp black mustard seeds
2.5ml/½ tsp cumin seeds
1 onion, thinly sliced
2 curry leaves
1 fresh green chilli, finely chopped
2.5cm/1in piece fresh root ginger, finely chopped
30ml/2 tbsp curry paste
1 small cauliflower, broken into florets
1 large carrot, thickly sliced
115g/4oz green beans, cut into 2.5cm/1in lengths
1.5ml/¼ tsp ground turmeric
1.5ml/¼ tsp chilli powder
2.5ml/½ tsp salt
2 tomatoes, finely chopped
50g/2oz/½ cup frozen peas, thawed
150ml/¼ pint/⅔ cup vegetable stock
fresh curry leaves, to garnish

1 Heat the oil in a large, heavy pan and fry the mustard seeds and cumin seeds for 2 minutes until they begin to splutter. If they are very lively, put a lid on the pan.

2 Add the onion and the curry leaves and fry for 5 minutes.

3 Add the chopped chilli and fresh ginger and fry for 2 minutes. Stir in the curry paste, mix well and fry for 3–4 minutes.

4 Add the cauliflower florets, sliced carrot and beans, and cook for 4–5 minutes. Add the turmeric, chilli powder, salt and tomatoes and cook for 2–3 minutes.

5 Finally add the thawed peas and cook for a further 2–3 minutes. Pour in the stock. Cover and simmer over a low heat for 10–15 minutes until all the vegetables are tender. Serve garnished with curry leaves.

Energy 130kcal/540kJ; Fat 6.2g; Saturated fat 0.61g; Carbohydrate 12.3g; Fibre 6.2g.

Vegetable Korma

Here the aim is to produce a subtle, aromatic curry rather than an assault on the senses.

Serves 4
50g/2oz/¼ cup butter
2 onions, sliced
2 garlic cloves, crushed
2.5cm/1in piece fresh root ginger, grated
5ml/1 tsp ground cumin
15ml/1 tbsp ground coriander
6 cardamom pods
5cm/2in piece of cinnamon stick
5ml/1 tsp ground turmeric
1 fresh red chilli, seeded and finely chopped
1 potato, peeled and cut into 2.5cm/1in cubes
1 small aubergine (eggplant), chopped
115g/4oz/1½ cups mushrooms, thickly sliced
175ml/6fl oz/¾ cup water
115g/4oz green beans, cut into 2.5cm/1in lengths
60ml/4 tbsp natural (plain) yogurt
150ml/¼ pint/⅔ cup double (heavy) cream
5ml/1 tsp garam masala
salt and ground black pepper
fresh coriander (cilantro) sprigs, to garnish
boiled rice and poppadums, to serve

1 Melt the butter in a heavy pan. Add the onions and cook for 5 minutes until soft. Add the garlic and ginger and cook for 2 minutes, then stir in the cumin, coriander, cardamom pods, cinnamon stick, turmeric and finely chopped chilli. Cook, stirring constantly, for 30 seconds.

2 Add the potato cubes, aubergine and mushrooms and the water. Cover the pan, bring to the boil, then lower the heat and simmer for 15 minutes.

3 Add the beans and cook, uncovered, for 5 minutes. With a slotted spoon, remove the vegetables to a warmed serving dish and keep hot.

4 Allow the cooking liquid to bubble up until it has reduced a little. Season with salt and pepper to taste, then stir in the yogurt, double cream and garam masala. Pour the sauce over the vegetables and garnish with fresh coriander. Serve with boiled rice and poppadums.

Energy 361kcal/1494kJ; Fat 31.3g; Saturated fat 19.3g; Carbohydrate 16.7g; Fibre 3.2g.

Spiced Vegetable Curry with Yogurt

This is a very delicately spiced vegetable dish that is particularly appetizing when served with plain yogurt. It is also a good accompaniment to a main course of heavily spiced curries.

Serves 4–6
350g/12oz mixed vegetables, such as beans, peas, potatoes, cauliflower, carrots, cabbage, mangetouts (snow peas) and mushrooms
30ml/2 tbsp vegetable oil
5ml/1 tsp cumin seeds, freshly roasted
2.5ml/½ tsp mustard seeds
2.5ml/½ tsp onion seeds
5ml/1 tsp ground turmeric
2 garlic cloves, crushed
6–8 curry leaves
1 dried red chilli
salt
5ml/1 tsp granulated sugar
150ml/¼ pint/⅔ cup natural (plain) yogurt mixed with 5ml/1 tsp cornflour (cornstarch)

1 Prepare all the vegetables you have chosen: string the beans; thaw the peas, if frozen; peel and cube the potatoes; cut the cauliflower into florets; dice the carrots; shred the cabbage; trim the mangetouts; wipe the mushrooms and leave whole.

2 Heat a large pan with enough water to cook all the vegetables and bring to the boil. First add the potatoes and carrots and cook until nearly tender then add all the other vegetables and cook until crisp-tender. All the vegetables should be crunchy except the potatoes. Drain.

3 Heat the oil in a frying pan and fry the cumin, mustard and onion seeds, the turmeric, garlic, curry leaves and dried chilli gently until the garlic is golden brown and the chilli nearly burnt. Reduce the heat.

4 Fold in the drained vegetables, add the sugar and salt and gradually add the yogurt and cornflour mixture. Heat until piping hot, and serve immediately.

Energy 99kcal/411kJ; Fat 6.1g; Saturated fat 0.9g; Carbohydrate 6.5g; Fibre 2g.

Vegetable Kashmiri

This is a wonderful vegetable curry, in which fresh mixed vegetables are cooked in a spicy aromatic yogurt sauce. The spicing is quite gentle, so it will appeal to most palates.

Serves 4
10ml/2 tsp cumin seeds
8 black peppercorns
seeds from 2 green cardamom pods
5cm/2in piece cinnamon stick
2.5ml/½ tsp grated nutmeg
30ml/2 tbsp oil
1 fresh green chilli, chopped
2.5cm/1in piece fresh root ginger, grated
5ml/1 tsp chilli powder
2.5ml/½ tsp salt
2 large potatoes, cut into 2.5cm/1in chunks
225g/8oz cauliflower, broken into florets
225g/8oz okra, trimmed and thickly sliced
150ml/¼ pint/⅔ cup natural (plain) low-fat yogurt
150ml/¼ pint/⅔ cup vegetable stock
toasted flaked (sliced) almonds and fresh coriander (cilantro) sprigs, to garnish

1 Grind the cumin seeds and peppercorns, cardamom seeds, cinnamon stick and nutmeg to a fine powder using a spice blender or a pestle and mortar.

2 Heat the oil in a large, heavy pan and fry the chilli and ginger for 2 minutes, stirring all the time.

3 Add the chilli powder, salt and ground spice mixture, and fry for about 2–3 minutes, stirring all the time to prevent the spices from sticking to the bottom of the pan.

4 Stir in the potatoes, cover and cook for 10 minutes over a low heat, stirring from time to time.

5 Add the cauliflower and okra and cook for 5 minutes.

6 Add the yogurt and stock. Bring to the boil, then reduce the heat. Cover and simmer for 20 minutes, or until all the vegetables are tender. Garnish with the toasted almonds and the coriander sprigs.

Energy 220kcal/920kJ; Fat 8.2g; Saturated fat 1.02g; Carbohydrate 29.1g; Fibre 4.7g.

Vegetable Biryani

This is a good-tempered dish made from everyday ingredients, and thus indispensable for the cook catering for an unexpected vegetarian guest.

Serves 4–6

175g/6oz/scant 1 cup long-grain rice, rinsed
2 whole cloves
seeds from 2 cardamom pods
450ml/³⁄₄ pint/scant 2 cups vegetable stock
2 garlic cloves
1 small onion, roughly chopped
5ml/1 tsp cumin seeds
5ml/1 tsp ground coriander
2.5ml/¹⁄₂ tsp ground turmeric
2.5ml/¹⁄₂ tsp chilli powder
1 large potato, cut into 2.5cm/1in cubes
2 carrots, sliced
¹⁄₂ cauliflower, broken into florets
50g/2oz green beans, cut into 2.5cm/1in lengths
30ml/2 tbsp chopped fresh coriander (cilantro), plus extra to garnish
30ml/2 tbsp lime juice
salt and ground black pepper

1 Put the rice, cloves and cardamom seeds into a large, heavy pan. Pour over the stock and bring to the boil. Reduce the heat, cover the pan and simmer for 20 minutes or until all the stock has been absorbed.

2 Meanwhile, put the garlic cloves, onion, cumin seeds, ground coriander, turmeric, chilli powder and seasoning into a blender or food processor together with 30ml/2 tbsp water. Blend to a smooth paste. Scrape the paste into a large flameproof casserole.

3 Preheat the oven to 180°C/350°F/Gas 4. Cook the spicy paste in the casserole over a low heat for 2 minutes, stirring occasionally. Add the potato cubes, carrots, cauliflower, beans and 90ml/6 tbsp water. Cover and cook over a low heat for 12 minutes, stirring occasionally. Add the chopped fresh coriander.

4 Remove the cloves from the rice. Spoon the rice over the vegetables. Sprinkle with the lime juice. Cover and cook in the oven for 25 minutes or until the vegetables are tender. Fluff up the rice with a fork before serving, garnished with coriander.

Broad Bean & Cauliflower Curry

This is a hot and spicy vegetable curry, tasty when served with cooked rice (especially a brown basmati variety), a few poppadums and cucumber raita.

Serves 4

2 garlic cloves, chopped
2.5cm/1in piece fresh root ginger
1 fresh green chilli, seeded and chopped
30ml/2 tbsp oil
1 onion, sliced
1 large potato, chopped
15ml/1 tbsp curry powder, mild or hot
1 cauliflower, cut into small florets
600ml/1 pint/2¹⁄₂ cups vegetable stock
275g/10oz can broad (fava) beans
juice of ¹⁄₂ lemon (optional)
salt and ground black pepper
fresh coriander (cilantro) sprig, to garnish
plain rice, to serve

1 Blend the chopped garlic, ginger, chopped chilli and 15ml/1 tbsp of the oil in a food processor or blender until the mixture forms a smooth paste.

2 In a large, heavy pan, fry the sliced onion and chopped potato in the remaining oil for 5 minutes, then stir in the spice paste and curry powder. Cook for another minute.

3 Add the cauliflower florets to the onion and potato and stir well until they are thoroughly combined with the spicy mixture, then pour in the stock and bring to the boil over medium to high heat.

4 Season well, cover and simmer for 10 minutes. Add the beans with the liquid from the can and cook, uncovered, for a further 10 minutes.

5 Check the seasoning and adjust if necessary. Add a good squeeze of lemon juice, if you like, and serve hot, garnished with coriander and accompanied by plain boiled rice.

Energy 260kcal/1100kJ Fat 1.9g Saturated fat 0.07g Carbohydrate 55.8g Fibre 3.2g.

Energy 216kcal/906kJ; Fat 7.7g; Saturated fat 0.75g; Carbohydrate 25.8g; Fibre 7.9g.

Spicy Chickpea & Aubergine Stew

Aubergines and chickpeas go particularly well with the warm spices in this substantial dish.

Serves 4

3 garlic cloves
2 large onions
3 large aubergines (eggplants), cubed
200g/7oz/1 cup chickpeas, soaked overnight
60ml/4 tbsp olive oil
2.5ml/ ½ tsp ground cumin
2.5ml/ ½ tsp ground cinnamon
2.5ml/ ½ tsp ground coriander
3 x 400g/14oz cans chopped tomatoes
salt and ground black pepper
boiled rice, to serve

For the garnish

30ml/2 tbsp olive oil
1 onion, sliced
1 garlic clove, sliced
sprigs of fresh coriander (cilantro)

1 Chop the garlic and onions and set aside. Cut the aubergines into bitesize cubes.

2 Place the aubergine cubes in a colander and sprinkle them with salt. Sit the colander in a bowl and leave for 30 minutes, to allow the bitter juices to escape. Rinse the aubergine with cold water and dry on kitchen paper.

3 Drain the chickpeas and put in a pan with enough water to cover. Bring to the boil and simmer for 1–1½ hours, or until tender. Drain.

4 Heat the oil in a large pan. Add the garlic and onion, and cook until soft. Add the spices and cook, stirring, for a few seconds. Add the aubergine and stir. Cook for 5 minutes.

5 Add the tomatoes and chickpeas and season with salt and pepper. Cover and simmer for 20 minutes.

6 To make the garnish, heat the oil in a frying pan and, when very hot, add the sliced onion and garlic. Fry until golden and crisp. Serve the stew with rice, topped with the onion and garlic and garnished with coriander.

Energy 384kcal/1613kJ; Fat 15.8g; Saturated fat 2.4g; Carbohydrate 47.5g; Fibre 14.8g.

Masala Chana

Chickpeas are used and cooked in a variety of ways all over the Indian subcontinent. Tamarind adds a sharp, tangy flavour.

Serves 4

225g/8oz/1¼ cups dried chickpeas, soaked overnight and drained
50g/2oz tamarind stick
120ml/4fl oz/½ cup boiling water
30ml/2 tbsp oil
2.5ml/½ tsp cumin seeds
1 onion, finely chopped
2 garlic cloves, crushed
2.5cm/1 in piece fresh root ginger, grated
1 fresh green chilli, finely chopped
5ml/1 tsp ground cumin
5ml/1 tsp ground coriander
1.5ml/¼ tsp ground turmeric
2.5ml/½ tsp salt
225g/8oz tomatoes, peeled and finely chopped
2.5ml/½ tsp garam masala
chopped fresh chillies and chopped onion, to garnish

1 Place the chickpeas in a large pan with double the volume of cold water. Bring to the boil and boil vigorously for 10 minutes.

2 Skim off any scum that has risen to the surface of the liquid, using a slotted spoon. Lower the heat, cover the pan and simmer for 1½–2 hours or until the chickpeas are soft.

3 Meanwhile, break up the tamarind and soak in the boiling water for about 15 minutes. Rub the tamarind through a sieve into a bowl, discarding any stones and fibre left behind.

4 Heat the oil in a large, heavy pan and fry the cumin seeds for 2 minutes until they splutter. Add the onion, garlic, ginger and chilli, and fry for 5 minutes.

5 Stir in the cumin and coriander, with the turmeric and salt and fry for 3–4 minutes. Add the chopped tomatoes. Bring to the boil and then simmer for 5 minutes.

6 Drain the chickpeas and add to the tomato mixture together with the garam masala and tamarind pulp. Cover and simmer gently for about 15 minutes. Garnish with the chopped chillies and onion before serving.

Energy 313kcal/1317kJ; Fat 9.4g; Saturated fat 0.77g; Carbohydrate 44.6g; Fibre 1.5g.

Black-eyed Beans & Potato Curry

Nutty-flavoured black-eyed beans make a nutritious supper dish, especially when mixed with potatoes. This hot and spicy combination will be ideal for an autumn or winter evening.

Serves 4–6

2 potatoes
225g/8oz/1¼ cups black-eyed beans (peas), soaked overnight and drained
1.5ml/¼ tsp bicarbonate of soda (baking soda)
5ml/1 tsp five-spice powder
1.5ml/¼ tsp asafoetida
2 onions, finely chopped
2.5cm/1in piece fresh root ginger, crushed
a few fresh mint leaves
450ml/¾ pint/scant 2 cups water
60ml/4 tbsp vegetable oil
2.5ml/½ tsp each ground cumin, ground coriander, ground turmeric and chilli powder
4 fresh green chillies, chopped
75ml/5 tbsp tamarind juice
115g/4oz/4 cups fresh coriander (cilantro), chopped
2 firm tomatoes, chopped
salt

1 Cut the potatoes into cubes and boil in lightly salted water until tender.

2 Place the drained black-eyed beans in a heavy pan and add the bicarbonate of soda, five-spice powder and asafoetida. Add the chopped onions, crushed root ginger, mint leaves and the measured water. Simmer until the beans are soft. Remove any excess water and reserve.

3 Heat the oil in a frying pan. Gently fry the ground cumin and coriander, the turmeric and chilli powder with the green chillies and tamarind juice, until they are well blended.

4 Pour the spice mixture over the black-eyed beans and mix well.

5 Add the potatoes, fresh coriander, tomatoes and salt. Mix well, and, if necessary, thin with a little reserved water. Reheat and serve.

Boiled Egg Curry

This dish can be served on its own, or it makes a good accompaniment to a biryani or pilau.

Serves 3–6

10ml/2 tsp white poppy seeds
10ml/2 tsp white sesame seeds
10ml/2 tsp whole coriander seeds
30ml/2 tbsp desiccated (dry unsweetened shredded) coconut
350ml/½fl oz/1½ cups tomato juice
10ml/2 tsp gram flour
5ml/1 tsp crushed fresh root ginger
5ml/1 tsp chilli powder
1.5ml/¼ tsp asafoetida
salt
5ml/1 tsp sugar
6 hard-boiled eggs, halved
30ml/2 tbsp sesame oil
5ml/1 tsp cumin seeds
4 dried red chillies
6–8 curry leaves
4 garlic cloves, finely sliced

1 Heat a frying pan and dry-fry the poppy, sesame and coriander seeds for 3–4 minutes. Add the desiccated coconut and dry-fry until it browns.

2 Cool and grind the ingredients together using a pestle and mortar or a food processor.

3 Take a little of the tomato juice and mix with the gram flour to a smooth paste. Add the ginger, chilli powder, asafoetida, salt and sugar and the ground spices. Add the remaining tomato juice, place in a pan and simmer gently for 10 minutes.

4 Add the hard-boiled eggs and cover with the sauce. Heat the oil in a frying pan and fry the remaining ingredients until the chillies turn dark brown. Pour the spices and oil over the egg curry, fold the ingredients together and reheat. Serve hot.

> **Cook's Tip**
> Gram flour, or besan, is made from ground chickpeas. It is less starchy than wheat flour and is used extensively in Indian cooking. For a recipe like this that uses a very tiny amount as a thickener, plain (all-purpose) flour can be substituted.

Energy 362kcal/1526kJ; Fat 12.4g; Saturated fat 1.6g; Carbohydrate 49.6g; Fibre 6.6g.

Energy 344kcal/1430kJ; Fat 28.5g; Saturated fat 10.1g; Carbohydrate 7g; Fibre 2.6g.

Eggs on Chipsticks

This is an unusual and delicious way of combining eggs with potato sticks, and is known as *sali pur eeda* in the Parsee language. The potato sticks are fried with chillies, turmeric and coriander. Eggs are then broken over the top and cooked until just set. It makes an unusual light lunch or supper dish and is incredibly quick to prepare and cook.

Serves 4–6

225g/8oz salted chipsticks
2 fresh green chillies, finely chopped
a few coriander (cilantro) sprigs, chopped
1.5ml/ 1/4 tsp ground turmeric
60ml/4 tbsp vegetable oil
75ml/5 tbsp water
6 eggs
3 spring onions (scallions), finely chopped
salt and ground black pepper

1 In a large bowl, mix the salted chipsticks with the chopped chillies, coriander and turmeric.

2 Heat 30ml/2 tbsp of the oil in a heavy frying pan. Add the chipstick mixture and water. Cook until the chipsticks turn soft, and then crisp.

3 Place a dinner plate over the frying pan, and hold in place as you turn the pan over and carefully transfer the chipstick "pancake" on to the plate. Heat the remaining oil in the pan and slide the "pancake" back into the frying pan to brown the other side. Do this very gently, so that no chipsticks break off.

4 Gently break the eggs over the top, cover the frying pan and leave the eggs to set over a low heat. Season well and sprinkle with spring onions. Cook until the base is crisp. Serve hot for breakfast in the Parsee style, or with chapatis and a salad for lunch or supper.

> **Cook's Tip**
> As the chipsticks cook, the starch they contain will cause them to stick together. To encourage this, use a spoon to press them down.

Spicy Omelette

Another popular contribution by the Parsees, this irresistible omelette of potato, peas and corn is known to them as *poro*. Parsee cuisine offers some unique flavours, which appeal to both Eastern and Western palates.

Serves 4–6

30ml/2 tbsp vegetable oil
1 onion, finely chopped
2.5ml/ 1/2 tsp ground cumin
1 garlic clove, crushed
1 or 2 fresh green chillies, finely chopped
a few coriander (cilantro) sprigs, chopped, plus extra, to garnish
1 firm tomato, chopped
1 small potato, cubed and boiled
25g/1oz/ 1/4 cup cooked peas
25g/1oz/ 1/4 cup cooked corn, or drained canned corn
2 eggs, beaten
25g/1oz/ 1/4 cup grated Cheddar cheese or Monterey Jack
salt and ground black pepper

1 Heat the oil in a karahi, wok or omelette pan, and add the onion, cumin, garlic, chillies, coriander, tomato, potato, peas and corn. Mix well.

2 Cook over a medium heat, stirring, for 5 minutes, until the potato and tomato are almost tender. Season well.

3 Preheat the grill (broiler) to high. Increase the heat under the pan and pour in the beaten eggs. Reduce the heat, cover and cook until the bottom layer is brown. Turn the omelette over and sprinkle with the grated cheese. Place under the hot grill and cook until the egg sets and the cheese has melted.

4 Garnish the omelette with sprigs of coriander and serve with salad for a light lunch. If you prefer, serve it for breakfast, in the typical Parsee style.

> **Variation**
> You can use any vegetable with the potatoes. Try thickly sliced button (white) mushrooms, which can be added in step 1.

Energy 482kcal/2008kJ; Fat 33.3g; Saturated fat 6.8g; Carbohydrate 36.6g; Fibre 1.6g.

Energy 167kcal/694kJ; Fat 11.3g; Saturated fat 3g; Carbohydrate 9.7g; Fibre 1.5g.

Scrambled Eggs with Chilli

This is a lovely way to liven up scrambled eggs. Prepare all the ingredients ahead so that the vegetables can be cooked quickly and retain crunch and colour.

Serves 4
30ml/2 tbsp sunflower oil
1 onion, finely sliced
225g/8oz Chinese leaves
  (Chinese cabbage), finely sliced
  or cut in diamonds
200g/7oz can corn
1 small fresh red chilli, seeded
  and finely sliced
30ml/2 tbsp water
2 eggs, beaten
salt and ground black pepper
deep-fried onions, to garnish

1 Heat a karahi, wok or deep pan. Add the oil and, when it is hot, fry the onion until soft but not browned.

2 Add the Chinese leaves and toss the mixture over the heat until well mixed.

3 Add the corn, chilli and water. Cover with a lid and cook for 2 minutes.

4 Remove the lid and stir in the beaten eggs and seasoning. Stir constantly until the eggs are creamy and just set. Serve on warmed plates, sprinkled with crisp deep-fried onions.

Variations
• Chinese leaves give this dish a delicate flavour, which complements the corn and eggs well, but you could substitute other vegetables for a different flavour and appearance.
• Instead of Chinese leaves, you could try finely shredded spring greens (collards) or white cabbage. A mandolin is a useful implement for finely shredding vegetables such as these.
• Red, green or yellow (bell) peppers could also be used in place of the Chinese leaves and give the dish a bright appearance.

Purée of Lentils with Baked Eggs

This unusual dish of brown lentils spiced with coriander and mint makes an excellent supper. For a nutty flavour you could add a 400g/14oz can of unsweetened chestnut purée to the lentil mixture.

Serves 4
450g/1lb/2 cups washed
  brown lentils
3 leeks, thinly sliced
10ml/2 tsp coriander seeds,
  crushed
15ml/1 tbsp chopped fresh
  coriander (cilantro)
30ml/2 tbsp chopped fresh mint
15ml/1 tbsp red wine vinegar
1 litre/1¾ pints/4 cups vegetable
  stock
4 eggs
salt and ground black pepper
generous handful of fresh parsley,
  chopped, to garnish

1 Put the lentils in a deep pan. Add the leeks, coriander seeds, fresh coriander, mint, vinegar and stock. Bring to the boil, then lower the heat and simmer for 30–40 minutes, until the lentils are cooked and have absorbed all the liquid.

2 Preheat the oven to 180°C/350°F/Gas 4.

3 Season the lentils with salt and pepper, and mix well. Spread out in four lightly greased baking dishes.

4 Using the back of a spoon, make a hollow in the lentil mixture in each dish. Break an egg into each hollow. Cover the dishes with foil and bake for 15–20 minutes, or until the egg whites are set and the yolks are still soft. Sprinkle with plenty of parsley and serve at once.

Cook's Tip
If you prefer, the lentil mixture can be put into a large dish. Make four indentations in the mixture to hold the eggs.

Energy 171kcal/711kJ; Fat 10.3g; Saturated fat 1.8g; Carbohydrate 13.7g; Fibre 2.1g.

Energy 470kcal/1990kJ; Fat 7.9g; Saturated fat 1.9g; Carbohydrate 68.4g; Fibre 8.8g.

Plain Boiled Rice

Always use basmati rice for the best flavour and texture. It is easy to cook and produces an excellent finished result. It is slimmer than other long grain rice and has a delicate flavour. Although slightly more expensive, it is well worth buying as it is the perfect rice for accompanying curries.

Serves 4–6
150ml/1 tbsp ghee, unsalted (sweet) butter or olive oil
350g/12oz/1¾ cups basmati rice, washed and drained
450ml/¾ pint/scant 2 cups water
salt

1 Rinse the basmati rice well in cold water until most of the starch is removed and the water runs clear.

2 Heat the ghee, butter or oil in a pan and sauté the drained rice thoroughly for about 2–3 minutes.

3 Add the water and salt and bring to the boil. Reduce the heat to low, cover and cook gently for 10–15 minutes. To serve, fluff the grains gently with a fork.

Cook's Tips
• *Always test the rice after it has cooked for about 10 minutes; it should be just cooked.*
• *As a guide, 75g/3oz/scant ½ cup raw rice will give you an ample helping for one person.*

Variation
To make a fragrantly spiced version, sauté 4–6 green cardamom pods, 4 cloves, 5cm/2in piece cinnamon stick, 2.5ml/½ tsp black cumin seeds and 2 bay leaves. Add 350g/12oz/1¾ cups drained basmati rice and proceed as for plain boiled rice. For an even more luxurious rice, add 6–8 strands of saffron and sauté with the spices.

Energy 342kcal/1429kJ; Fat 3.5g; Saturated fat 2g; Carbohydrate 69.9g; Fibre 0g.

Indian Pilau Rice

This traditional spiced rice is the perfect accompaniment for vegetarian dishes.

Serves 4
225g/8oz/1¼ cups basmati rice
15ml/1 tbsp oil
1 small onion, finely chopped
1 garlic clove, crushed
5ml/1 tsp fennel seeds
15ml/1 tbsp sesame seeds
2.5ml/½ tsp ground turmeric
5ml/1 tsp ground cumin
1.5ml/¼ tsp salt
2 whole cloves
4 cardamom pods, lightly crushed
5 black peppercorns
450ml/¾ pint/scant 2 cups vegetable stock
fresh coriander (cilantro), to garnish

1 Wash the rice well and leave to soak in water for 30 minutes. Heat the oil in a heavy pan, add the onion and garlic and fry gently for 5–6 minutes until softened.

2 Stir in the fennel and sesame seeds, the turmeric, cumin, salt, cloves, cardamom pods and peppercorns and fry for about a minute. Drain the rice well, add to the pan and stir-fry for a further 3 minutes.

3 Pour on the vegetable stock. Bring to the boil, then cover. Reduce the heat to very low and simmer gently for 20 minutes, without removing the lid, until all the liquid has been absorbed.

4 Remove from the heat and leave to stand for 2–3 minutes. Fluff up the rice with a fork, garnish with coriander and transfer to a warmed dish to serve.

Cook's Tip
In South India, where large quantities of rice are eaten, people prefer a rice which will absorb the spicy flavours of seasonings. In this recipe, basmati rice is cooked in the traditional way to seal in all the flavour.

Energy 265kcal/1108kJ Fat 6g Saturated fat 0.68g Carbohydrate 49.5g Fibre 0.6g.

Colourful Pilau Rice

This lightly spiced rice makes an extremely attractive accompaniment to many Balti dishes, and is easily made.

Serves 4–6

450g/1lb/2¹/₃ cups basmati
  rice
75g/3oz/6 tbsp unsalted
  (sweet) butter

4 cloves
4 green cardamom pods
1 bay leaf
5ml/1 tsp salt
1 litre/1³/₄ pints/4 cups water
a few drops each of yellow, green
  and red food colouring

1 Wash the basmati rice twice, drain well and set aside in a sieve (strainer).

2 Melt the butter in a medium pan, and add the cloves, cardamoms, bay leaf and salt. Lower the heat and add the rice. Fry for about 1 minute, stirring constantly.

3 Add the water to the rice and spices and bring to the boil. As soon as it has boiled, cover the pan and reduce the heat. Cook for 10–15 minutes. Taste a grain of rice after 10 minutes; it should be slightly *al dente* (soft but with a bite in the centre).

4 Just before you are ready to serve the rice, pour a few drops of each colouring at different sides of the pan. Leave to stand for 5 minutes so that the colours can "bleed" into the rice. Mix gently with a fork and serve.

> **Variation**
> *For Nut Pilau, fry 1.5ml/1/4 tsp cumin seeds with the cloves and cardamoms at step 2. When the rice has almost cooked, drain it and gently stir in a pinch of saffron threads and 15ml/ 1 tbsp ground almonds. Leave the rice to stand for a few minutes before serving. Omit the food colouring.*

Energy 544kcal/2263kJ; Fat 16g; Saturated fat 9.8g; Carbohydrate 89.9g; Fibre 0g.

Fruity Pilau

Sultanas and almonds make this a flavoursome rice to serve alongside rich curries.

Serves 4–6

450g/1lb/2¹/₃ cups basmati
  rice
75g/3oz/6 tbsp unsalted
  (sweet) butter
15ml/1 tbsp corn oil

1 bay leaf
6 black peppercorns
4 green cardamom pods
5ml/1 tsp salt
75g/3oz/¹/₂ cup sultanas
  (golden raisins)
50g/2oz/¹/₂ cup flaked
  (sliced) almonds
1 litre/1³/₄ pints/4 cups
  water

1 Wash the basmati rice twice, drain well and set aside in a sieve (strainer).

2 Heat the butter and oil in a medium pan. Lower the heat and throw in the bay leaf, peppercorns and cardamoms, and fry for about 30 seconds.

3 Add the rice, salt, sultanas and flaked almonds. Stir-fry for about 1 minute, then pour in the water. Bring to the boil, then cover with a tightly fitting lid and lower the heat. Cook for 15–20 minutes. Taste a grain of rice after 10 minutes; it should be slightly *al dente* (soft but with a bite in the centre).

4 Turn off the heat and leave the rice to stand, still covered, for about 5 minutes. The rice will continue cooking gently during this time. Serve.

> **Variation**
> *For Mushroom Pilau, boil the rice without any of the flavourings for 15 minutes and then drain. Stir-fry 10ml/2 tsp cumin seeds, 1.5ml/¹/₂ tsp fennel seeds and 1 star anise for 30 seconds. Add half a chopped onion and 75g/3oz/1 cup sliced mushrooms, and cook over medium-high heat for 5 minutes. Add to the rice and transfer to a casserole. Heat in the oven at 190°C/ 375°F/Gas 5 for 30 minutes.*

Energy 696kcal/2901kJ; Fat 25.8g; Saturated fat 10.7g; Carbohydrate 103.8g; Fibre 1.3g.

Nut Pilau

Versions of this rice dish are cooked throughout Asia, always with the best-quality long grain rice. In India, basmati rice is the natural choice. In this particular interpretation of the recipe, walnuts and cashew nuts are added. Serve the pilau with a raita or yogurt.

Serves 4

15–30ml/1–2 tbsp vegetable oil
1 onion, chopped
1 garlic clove, crushed
1 large carrot, coarsely grated
225g/8oz/generous 1 cup
　basmati rice, soaked for
　20–30 minutes
5ml/1 tsp cumin seeds
10ml/2 tsp ground coriander
10ml/2 tsp black mustard seeds
4 green cardamom pods
450ml/³⁄₄ pint/scant 2 cups
　vegetable stock
1 bay leaf
75g/3oz/³⁄₄ cup unsalted walnuts
　and cashew nuts
salt and ground black pepper
fresh coriander (cilantro) sprigs,
　to garnish

1 Heat the oil in a karahi, wok or large pan. Fry the onion, garlic and carrot for 3–4 minutes. Drain the rice and add to the pan with the spices. Cook for 2 minutes, stirring to coat the grains in oil.

2 Pour in the stock, stirring. Add the bay leaf and season well.

3 Bring to the boil, lower the heat, cover and simmer very gently for 10–12 minutes without stirring.

4 Remove the pan from the heat without lifting the lid. Leave to stand for 5 minutes, then check the rice. If it is cooked, there will be small steam holes on the surface of the rice. Discard the bay leaf and the cardamom pods.

5 Stir in the walnuts and cashew nuts and check the seasoning. Spoon on to a warmed platter, garnish with the fresh coriander and serve.

Energy 376kcal/1562kJ; Fat 16g; Saturated fat 1.4g; Carbohydrate 50g; Fibre 1.6g.

Sultana & Cashew Pilau

The secret of a perfect pilau is to wash the rice thoroughly, then soak it briefly. This softens and moistens the grains, enabling the rice to absorb moisture during cooking, which results in fluffier rice.

Serves 4

600ml/1 pint/2¹⁄₂ cups hot
　vegetable stock
generous pinch of saffron threads
50g/2oz/¹⁄₄ cup butter
1 onion, chopped
1 garlic clove, crushed
2.5cm/1in piece cinnamon stick
6 green cardamom pods
1 bay leaf
250g/9oz/1¹⁄₃ cups basmati
　rice, soaked in water for
　20–30 minutes
50g/2oz/¹⁄₃ cup sultanas
　(golden raisins)
15ml/1 tbsp vegetable oil
50g/2oz/¹⁄₂ cup cashew nuts
naan bread and tomato and
　onion salad, to serve

1 Pour the hot vegetable stock into a jug (pitcher). Stir in the saffron threads and set aside.

2 Heat the butter in a pan and fry the onion and garlic for 5 minutes. Stir in the cinnamon stick, cardamoms and bay leaf and cook for 2 minutes.

3 Drain the rice and add to the pan, then cook, stirring, for 2 minutes more. Pour in the saffron stock and add the sultanas. Bring to the boil, stir, then lower the heat, cover and cook gently for 10 minutes or until the rice is tender and all the liquid has been absorbed.

4 Meanwhile, heat the oil in a wok, karahi or large pan and fry the cashew nuts until browned. Drain on kitchen paper, then sprinkle the cashew nuts over the rice. Serve with naan bread and tomato and onion salad.

Cook's Tip
Saffron powder can be used instead of saffron threads, if you prefer. Dissolve it in the hot stock.

Energy 462kcal/1922kJ Fat 19.5g Saturated fat 8g Carbohydrate 63.9g Fibre 1.2g.

Herby Rice Pilau

A quick and easy recipe to make, this simple pilau is delicious to eat. Serve with a main course vegetarian curry accompanied by a selection of fresh seasonal vegetables such as broccoli florets, baby corn, asparagus and carrots.

Serves 4

1 onion
1 garlic clove
225g/8oz/generous 1 cup mixed
   brown basmati and wild rice
15ml/1 tbsp olive oil
5ml/1 tsp ground cumin
5ml/1 tsp ground turmeric
50g/2oz/⅓ cup sultanas
   (golden raisins)
750ml/1¼ pints/3 cups vegetable
   stock
30–45ml/2–3 tbsp chopped
   fresh mixed herbs
salt and ground black pepper
sprigs of fresh herbs and 25g/
   1oz/¼ cup pistachio nuts,
   chopped, to garnish

1 Chop the onion and crush the garlic cloves.

2 Wash the rice under cold running water until the water runs clear, then drain well.

3 Heat the oil, add the onion and garlic, and cook gently for 5 minutes, stirring occasionally.

4 Add the ground cumin and turmeric and drained rice and cook gently for 1 minute, stirring. Stir in the sultanas and vegetable stock, bring to the boil, cover and simmer gently for 20–25 minutes, stirring occasionally.

5 Stir in the chopped mixed herbs and season with salt and pepper to taste.

6 Spoon the pilau into a warmed serving dish and garnish with fresh herb sprigs and a sprinkling of chopped pistachio nuts. Serve immediately.

Tomato & Spinach Pilau

This healthy recipe is both a tasty and nourishing dish for vegetarians.

Serves 4

225g/8oz/generous 1 cup brown
   basmati rice
30ml/2 tbsp vegetable oil
15ml/1 tbsp ghee or unsalted
   (sweet) butter
1 onion, chopped
2 garlic cloves, crushed
3 tomatoes, peeled and chopped
10ml/2 tsp dhana jeera powder,
   or 5ml/1 tsp ground coriander
   and 5ml/1 tsp ground cumin
2 carrots, coarsely grated
900ml/1½ pints/3¾ cups
   vegetable stock
275g/10oz young spinach leaves
50g/2oz/½ cup unsalted
   cashew nuts
salt and ground black pepper
naan bread, to serve

1 Wash the basmati rice. Place it in a bowl, cover with cold water and leave to soak for 20 minutes. Drain the rice and place it in a large pan of boiling salted water, bring back to the boil and cook for 10 minutes.

2 Heat the oil and ghee or butter in a karahi, wok or large pan, and fry the onion and garlic for 4–5 minutes until soft. Add the tomatoes and cook for 3–4 minutes, stirring, until the mixture thickens. Drain the rice, add it to the pan and cook for a further 1–2 minutes, stirring, until the grains of rice are coated.

3 Stir in the dhana jeera powder or coriander and cumin, then add the carrots. Season with salt and pepper. Pour in the stock and stir well to mix.

4 Bring to the boil, then cover tightly and simmer over a very gentle heat for 20–25 minutes, until the rice is tender.

5 Lay the spinach on the surface of the rice, cover again, and cook for a further 2–3 minutes, until the spinach has wilted. Fold the spinach into the rest of the rice.

6 Dry-fry the cashew nuts until lightly browned and sprinkle over the rice mixture. Serve with naan bread.

Energy 271kcal/1133kJ; Fat 3.3g; Saturated fat 0.4g; Carbohydrate 55.1g; Fibre 1.1g.

Energy 402kcal/1687kJ Fat 17.1g Saturated fat 4.4g Carbohydrate 56.4g Fibre 4.8g.

Saffron Rice

The saffron crocus is a perennial bulb that flowers for only two weeks of the year, and each stigma has to be removed by hand and dried with care. Consequently, saffron is said to be worth its weight in gold. Kashmir in the northern region of India is a major producer, so it isn't surprising that the subcontinent has some wonderful recipes for this beautifully fragrant spice.

Serves 6
450g/1lb/2⅓ cups basmati
   rice
750ml/1¼ pints/3 cups water
3 green cardamom pods
2 cloves
5ml/1 tsp salt
45ml/3 tbsp semi-skimmed
   (low-fat) milk
2.5ml/½ tsp saffron threads,
   crushed

1 Wash the rice, put it in a bowl and pour over water to cover. Leave to soak for 20 minutes.

2 Drain the basmati rice and put it in a large pan with the measured water. Add the cardamoms, cloves and salt. Stir, then bring to the boil. Lower the heat, cover the pan tightly, and simmer for 5 minutes.

3 Meanwhile, place the milk in a small pan. Add the saffron threads and heat through gently.

4 Pour the saffron milk over the rice and stir. Cover again and continue cooking over a low heat for 5–6 minutes.

5 Remove the pan from the heat without lifting the lid. Leave the rice to stand for about 5 minutes, then fork through just before serving.

> **Cook's Tip**
> *Washing and soaking the rice before cooking makes it fluffier.*

Tricolour Pilau

Most Indian restaurants in the West serve this popular vegetable pilau, which has three different vegetables. The effect is easily achieved with canned or frozen vegetables, but for entertaining or a special occasion dinner, you may prefer to use fresh produce.

Serves 4–6
225g/8oz/generous 1 cup
   basmati rice
30ml/2 tbsp vegetable
   oil
2.5ml/½ tsp cumin seeds
2 dried bay leaves
4 green cardamom pods
4 cloves
1 onion, finely chopped
1 carrot, finely diced
50g/2oz/½ cup frozen peas,
   thawed
50g/2oz/⅓ cup frozen corn,
   thawed
25g/1oz/¼ cup cashew nuts,
   lightly fried
475ml/16fl oz/2 cups water
1.5ml/¼ tsp ground cumin
salt

1 Wash the rice, then soak it in cold water for 20 minutes.

2 Heat the oil in a karahi, wok, or large pan over a medium heat, and fry the cumin seeds for 2 minutes. Add the bay leaves, cardamoms and cloves, and fry gently for 2 minutes more, stirring the spices from time to time.

3 Add the onion and fry until lightly browned. Stir in the diced carrot and cook, stirring, for 3–4 minutes.

4 Drain the soaked basmati rice and add to the contents in the pan. Stir well to mix. Add the peas, corn and fried cashew nuts.

5 Add the measured water and the ground cumin, and stir in salt to taste. Bring to the boil, cover and simmer for 15 minutes over a low heat until all the water is absorbed.

6 Leave to stand, covered, for 10 minutes. Fluff up the rice with a fork, transfer to a warmed dish and serve.

Energy 273kcal/1141kJ Fat 0.5g Saturated fat 0.1g Carbohydrate 60.2g Fibre 0g.

Energy 331kcal/1378kJ Fat 9.4g Saturated fat 1.4g Carbohydrate 54.1g Fibre 2g.

Pea & Mushroom Pilau

Tiny white mushrooms and petits pois, or baby peas, look great in this delectable rice dish.

Serves 6

450g/1lb/2¼ cups basmati rice
15ml/1 tbsp oil
2.5ml/½ tsp cumin seeds
2 black cardamom pods
2 cinnamon sticks
3 garlic cloves, sliced
5ml/1 tsp salt
1 medium tomato, sliced
50g/2oz/⅔ cup button (white) mushrooms
75g/3oz/¾ cup petits pois (baby peas)
750ml/1¼ pints/3 cups water

1 Wash the rice well and leave it to soak in water for 30 minutes.

2 In a medium, heavy pan, heat the oil and add the cumin seeds, cardamom, cinnamon sticks, garlic and salt.

3 Add the tomato and mushrooms and stir-fry for 2–3 minutes.

4 Tip the rice into a colander and drain it thoroughly. Add it to the pan with the peas. Stir gently, making sure that you do not break up the grains of rice.

5 Add the water and bring to the boil. Lower the heat, cover and continue to cook for 15–20 minutes. Just before serving, remove the lid from the pan and fluff up the rice with a fork. Spoon into a dish and serve immediately.

Cook's Tip
Petits pois are small green peas, picked when very young. The tender, sweet peas inside the immature pods are ideal for this delicately flavoured rice dish. However, if you can't find petits pois, garden peas can be used instead.

Rice with Seeds & Spices

Toasted sunflower and sesame seeds impart a rich, nutty flavour to rice spiced with turmeric, cardamom and coriander, for this delicious change from plain boiled rice, and a colourful accompaniment to serve with spicy curries. Basmati rice gives the best texture and flavour, but you can use ordinary long grain rice instead, if you prefer.

1 garlic clove, crushed
200g/7oz/1 cup basmati rice
400ml/14fl oz/1⅔ cups vegetable stock
115g/4oz/½ cup natural (plain) yogurt
15ml/1 tbsp toasted sunflower seeds
15ml/1 tbsp toasted sesame seeds
salt and ground black pepper
coriander (cilantro) leaves, to garnish

Serves 4

5ml/1 tsp sunflower oil
2.5ml/½ tsp ground turmeric
6 cardamom pods, lightly crushed
5ml/1 tsp coriander seeds, lightly crushed

1 Heat the oil in a non-stick frying pan and fry the turmeric, cardamom pods, coriander seeds and garlic for about 1 minute, stirring constantly.

2 Add the rice and stock, bring to the boil, then cover and simmer for 15 minutes, or until just tender.

3 Stir in the yogurt and the toasted sunflower and sesame seeds. Season with salt and pepper and serve hot, garnished with coriander leaves.

Cook's Tip
Seeds are particularly rich in minerals, so they are a good addition to all kinds of dishes. Light toasting will improve their fine flavour.

Energy 423kcal/1768kJ; Fat 3.8g; Saturated fat 0.39g; Carbohydrate 92.9g; Fibre 1.3g.

Energy 248kcal/1036kJ; Fat 5.4g; Saturated fat 0.7g; Carbohydrate 42.8g; Fibre 0.5g.

Basmati Rice with Potato

Rice is eaten at all meals in Indian and Pakistani homes. There are several ways of cooking rice, and mostly whole spices are used. Always choose a good-quality basmati rice.

Serves 4

300g/11oz/1½ cups basmati rice
15ml/1 tbsp oil
1 small cinnamon stick
1 bay leaf
1.5ml/¼ tsp black cumin seeds
3 green cardamom pods
1 medium onion, sliced
5ml/1 tsp grated fresh root ginger
5ml/1 tsp crushed garlic
1.5ml/¼ tsp ground turmeric
7.5ml/1½ tsp salt
1 large potato, roughly diced
475ml/16fl oz/2 cups water
15ml/1 tbsp chopped fresh coriander (cilantro)

1 Wash the rice well and leave it to soak in water for 20 minutes. Heat the oil in a heavy pan, add the cinnamon, bay leaf, black cumin seeds, cardamoms and onion and cook for about 2 minutes.

2 Add the ginger, garlic, turmeric, salt and potato, and cook for 1 minute.

3 Drain the rice thoroughly. Add it to the potato and spices in the pan.

4 Stir to mix, then pour in the water followed by the coriander. Cover the pan with a lid and cook for 15–20 minutes. Remove from the heat and leave to stand, still covered, for 5–10 minutes before serving.

> **Cook's Tip**
> *It is important to observe the standing time of this dish before serving. Use a slotted spoon to serve the rice and potato mixture and handle it gently to avoid breaking the delicate grains of rice.*

Basmati Rice & Peas with Curry Leaves

This is a very simple rice dish, but it is full of flavour and can make a useful quick main course.

Serves 4

300g/11oz/1½ cups basmati rice
15ml/1 tbsp oil
6–8 curry leaves
1.5ml/¼ tsp mustard seeds
1.5ml/¼ tsp onion seeds
30ml/2 tbsp fresh fenugreek leaves
5ml/1 tsp crushed garlic
5ml/1 tsp grated fresh root ginger
5ml/1 tsp salt
115g/4oz/1 cup frozen peas
475ml/16fl oz/2 cups water

1 Wash the rice well and leave it to soak in a bowl of water for 30 minutes.

2 Heat the oil in a heavy pan and add the curry leaves, mustard seeds, onion seeds, fenugreek leaves, garlic, ginger and salt and stir-fry for 2–3 minutes.

3 Drain the rice, add it to the pan and stir gently.

4 Add the frozen peas and water and bring to the boil. Lower the heat, cover with a lid and cook for 15–20 minutes. Remove from the heat and leave to stand, still covered, for 10 minutes.

5 When ready to serve, fluff up the rice with a fork. Spoon the mixture on to serving plates and serve immediately.

> **Cook's Tip**
> *Fenugreek is an important spice in Indian cuisine. It has a strong distinctive curry aroma while cooking and imparts a rich flavour to dishes. The leaves are available fresh and dried from Indian markets and stores, and are used sparingly in dishes, as the flavour is intense.*

Energy 371kcal/1572kJ Fat 5.72g Saturated fat 1.03g Carbohydrate 77.36g Fibre 1.62g.

Energy 336kcal/1425kJ; Fat 5.96g; Saturated fat 1.09g; Carbohydrate 67.67g; Fibre 1.83g.

Red Fried Rice

This vibrant rice dish owes its appeal as much to the bright colours of its ingredients – red onion, red pepper and cherry tomatoes – as it does to their flavours.

Serves 2
130g/4½oz/¾ cup basmati rice
30ml/2 tbsp groundnut (peanut) oil

1 small red onion, chopped
1 red (bell) pepper, seeded and chopped
225g/8oz cherry tomatoes, halved
2 eggs, beaten
salt and ground black pepper

1 Wash the rice several times under cold running water. Drain well.

2 Bring a large pan of water to the boil. Add the rice and cook for 10–12 minutes.

3 Meanwhile, heat the oil in a wok until very hot. Add the onion and red pepper and stir-fry for 2–3 minutes.

4 Add the cherry tomatoes and continue stir-frying for 2 minutes more.

5 Pour in the beaten eggs all at once. Cook for 30 seconds without stirring, then stir to break up the egg as it sets.

6 Drain the cooked rice thoroughly. Add to the wok and toss it over the heat with the vegetables and egg mixture for 3 minutes. Season with salt and pepper, and serve immediately.

> **Variation**
> *To add even more colour to this bright dish, you could replace the red (bell) pepper with an orange or green variety.*

Tomato Biryani

Although generally served as an accompaniment to a main course, this tasty rice dish can also be eaten as a complete meal on its own.

Serves 4
400g/14oz/2 cups basmati rice
15ml/1 tbsp oil
2.5ml/½ tsp onion seeds
1 medium onion, sliced

2 medium tomatoes, sliced
1 orange or yellow (bell) pepper, seeded and sliced
5ml/1 tsp grated fresh root ginger
5ml/1 tsp crushed garlic
5ml/1 tsp chilli powder
30ml/2 tbsp chopped fresh coriander (cilantro)
1 medium potato, diced
7.5ml/1½ tsp salt
50g/2oz/½ cup frozen peas
750ml/1¼ pints/3 cups water

1 Wash the rice well and leave it to soak in water for 30 minutes. Heat the oil in a heavy pan and fry the onion seeds for about 30 seconds. Add the sliced onion and fry for 5 minutes, stirring occasionally to prevent the slices from sticking to the pan.

2 Add the sliced tomatoes and peppers, ginger, garlic and chilli powder. Stir-fry for 2 minutes.

3 Add the fresh coriander, potato, salt and peas and stir-fry over a medium heat for a further 5 minutes.

4 Transfer the rice to a colander and drain it thoroughly. Add it to the spiced tomato and potato mixture and stir-fry for 1–2 minutes.

5 Pour in the water and bring to the boil, then lower the heat to medium. Cover and cook the rice for 12–15 minutes. Leave to stand for 5 minutes and then serve.

> **Cook's Tip**
> *Plain rice can look a bit dull; it is greatly enhanced by adding colourful ingredients such as tomatoes, peppers and peas.*

Energy 472kcal/1964kJ; Fat 17.3g; Saturated fat 2.9g; Carbohydrate 65.8g; Fibre 1.8g.

Energy 409kcal/1710kJ; Fat 3.7g; Saturated fat 0.44g; Carbohydrate 89.7g; Fibre 2.4g.

Tarka Dhal

Probably the most popular Indian lentil dish found today, Tarka Dhal is served in most Indian and Pakistani restaurants.

Serves 4
115g/4oz/½ cup masoor dhal
   (red split lentils)
50g/2oz/¼ cup mung dhal or
   yellow split peas
600ml/1 pint/2½ cups water
5ml/1 tsp grated fresh root ginger
5ml/1 tsp crushed garlic
1.5ml/¼ tsp ground turmeric
2 fresh green chillies, chopped
7.5ml/1½ tsp salt

For the tarka
30ml/2 tbsp oil
1 onion, sliced
1.5ml/¼ tsp mixed mustard
   and onion seeds
4 dried red chillies
1 tomato, sliced

For the garnish
15ml/1 tbsp chopped fresh
   coriander (cilantro)
1 or 2 fresh green chillies,
   seeded and sliced
15ml/1 tbsp chopped fresh
   mint

1 Boil all the masoor dhal and mung dhal or yellow split peas in the water with the ginger and garlic, turmeric and chopped green chillies for 15–20 minutes, or until soft.

2 Pound the mixture with a rolling pin or mash with a fork until it has a creamy consistency.

3 If the lentil mixture looks too dry, add a little more water. Season with the salt. To prepare the tarka, heat the oil in a heavy pan and fry the onion with the mustard and onion seeds, dried red chillies and tomato for 2 minutes.

4 Spoon the mashed lentils into a serving dish and pour the tarka over. Garnish with fresh coriander, green chillies and mint, and serve immediately.

> **Cook's Tip**
> Use 1 or 2 red chillies if you want a milder tarka for the dhal.

Energy 162kcal/681kJ Fat 6.6g Saturated fat 0.74g Carbohydrate 18.7g Fibre 3.2g.

Lentils Seasoned with Fried Spices

A simple supper dish for family or friends using traditional Indian lentils and peas.

Serves 4–6
115g/4oz/½ cup red gram
   (pigeon peas)
50g/2oz/¼ cup Bengal gram
4 fresh green chillies
5ml/1 tsp ground turmeric
1 large onion, sliced
400g/14oz can chopped tomatoes

60ml/4 tbsp vegetable oil
2.5ml/½ tsp mustard seeds
2.5ml/½ tsp cumin seeds
1 garlic clove, crushed
6 curry leaves
2 dried red chillies
salt
deep-fried onions and fresh
   coriander (cilantro),
   to garnish

1 Place the red gram and bengal gram in a heavy pan and pour in 350ml/12fl oz/1½ cups water. Add the chillies, turmeric and onion slices and bring to the boil. Simmer, covered, until the lentils are soft and the water has evaporated.

2 Mash the lentils with the back of a spoon. When nearly smooth, add the tomatoes and salt to taste, and mix well. If necessary, thin with a little hot water.

3 Heat the oil in a frying pan. Fry the remaining ingredients until the garlic browns. Pour the oil and spices over the lentils and cover. After 5 minutes, mix well, garnish, and serve.

> **Cook's Tips**
> • Red gram, or pigeon peas, are the fruit of a small shrub but are used as a vegetable. They form a staple food in India as well as Africa and the Caribbean, and you will find them in Asian and Caribbean stores and markets.
> • Bengal gram, or channa, is a small variety of chickpea, which is commonly used in Indian cuisine.

Energy 268kcal/1124kJ; Fat 11.8g; Saturated fat 1.4g; Carbohydrate 31g; Fibre 3.6g.

Green Lentils & Rice

Also known as continental lentils, green lentils retain their shape and colour when cooked. They are an important source of protein and add a robust flavour to dishes such as this. Chillies, ginger, cardamoms and cinnamon make this a lively main-course rice, excellent served with a vegetable curry or a simple salad.

Serves 4–6
350g/12oz/1¾ cups patna
    rice
175g/6oz/¾ cup green lentils
50g/2oz/¼ cup ghee
1 onion, finely chopped
2 garlic cloves, crushed
2.5cm/1in piece fresh root
    ginger, shredded
4 fresh green chillies,
    chopped
4 cloves
2.5cm/1in piece cinnamon stick
4 green cardamom pods
5ml/1 tsp ground turmeric
600ml/1 pint/2½ cups water
salt

1 Wash the rice and lentils, then soak them in a bowl of cold water for 20 minutes.

2 Gently heat the ghee in a large, heavy pan with a tight-fitting cover and fry the onion, garlic, ginger, chillies, cloves, cinnamon, cardamoms, turmeric and salt to taste until the onion is soft and translucent.

3 Drain the rice and lentils and add them to the spices in the pan. Sauté for 2–3 minutes. Add the water and bring the mixture to the boil.

4 Reduce the heat, cover and cook for about 20–25 minutes, or until all the water has been absorbed.

5 Take the pan off the heat and leave to rest with the lid on for 5 minutes.

6 Just before serving, gently toss the rice and lentils with a flat spatula, taking care not to break the delicate grains.

Energy 669kcal/2793kJ Fat 23.5g Saturated fat 15g Carbohydrate 97.4g Fibre 2.7g.

Courgettes with Split Lentils & Tomatoes

The nutty flavour of lentils goes particularly well with courgettes and tomatoes, perked up with a selection of aromatic spices. Serve with rice or bread for a filling and tasty supper.

Serves 4–6
225g/8oz courgettes (zucchini)
1 large onion, finely sliced
2 garlic cloves, crushed
2 fresh green chillies,
    chopped
175g/6oz/⅔ cup mung dhal
    or yellow split peas
2.5ml/½ tsp ground turmeric
60ml/4 tbsp vegetable oil
2.5ml/½ tsp mustard seeds
2.5ml/½ tsp cumin seeds
1.5ml/¼ tsp asafoetida
a few fresh coriander (cilantro)
    and mint leaves, chopped
6–8 curry leaves
2.5ml/½ tsp granulated sugar
200g/7oz can chopped tomatoes
60ml/4 tbsp lemon juice
salt

1 Cut the courgettes into wedges. Finely slice the onion and crush the garlic. Chop the green chillies.

2 In a pan, simmer the lentils and turmeric in 300ml/½ pint/1¼ cups water, until cooked but not mushy. Drain the cooked lentils, retaining the cooking liquid, and set aside while you cook the vegetables.

3 Heat the oil in a frying pan and add the courgette wedges, sliced onion, crushed garlic and chopped chillies. Add the mustard and cumin seeds, asafoetida, fresh coriander and mint, and stir in the curry leaves and sugar. Fry the ingredients together, stirring occasionally, and then add the chopped tomatoes. Mix well and add salt to taste.

4 Cover and cook until the courgettes are nearly tender but still crunchy.

5 Fold in the drained lentils and the lemon juice. If the dish is too dry, add some of the reserved cooking water. Reheat thoroughly and serve immediately.

Energy 278kcal/1165kJ Fat 12g Saturated fat 1.5g Carbohydrate 31.9g Fibre 3.9g.

Creamy Black Lentils

Black lentils, or urad dhal, are available whole, split, and skinned and split.

Serves 4–6

175g/6oz/³⁄₄ cup black lentils, soaked
50g/2oz/¹⁄₄ cup red split lentils
120ml/4fl oz/¹⁄₂ cup double (heavy) cream, plus extra to serve
120ml/4fl oz/¹⁄₂ cup natural (plain) yogurt
5ml/1 tsp cornflour (cornstarch)
40g/1¹⁄₂oz/3 tbsp ghee or vegetable oil
1 onion, finely chopped
5cm/2in piece fresh root ginger, crushed
4 fresh green chillies, chopped
1 tomato, chopped
2.5ml/¹⁄₂ tsp chilli powder
2.5ml/¹⁄₂ tsp ground turmeric
2.5ml/¹⁄₂ tsp ground cumin
2 garlic cloves, sliced
salt
coriander (cilantro) sprigs and sliced fresh red chilli, to garnish

1 Drain the black lentils and place in a large pan with the red lentils. Cover with water and bring to the boil. Reduce the heat, cover the pan and simmer until tender. Mash with a spoon, and cool.

2 In a bowl, mix together the cream, yogurt and cornflour, and stir into the lentils in the pan.

3 Heat 15g/¹⁄₂oz/1 tbsp of the ghee or oil in a karahi, wok or large pan, and fry the onion, ginger, half the green chillies and the tomato until the onion is soft.

4 Add the ground spices and salt, and fry for a further 2 minutes. Stir into the lentil mixture and mix well. Reheat, transfer to a heatproof serving dish and keep warm.

5 Heat the remaining ghee or oil in a frying pan over a low heat and fry the garlic slices and remaining chillies until the garlic slices are golden brown.

6 Pour over the lentils, and fold in the garlic and chilli just before serving. Garnish and serve with extra cream so that diners can add more as they eat, if they wish.

Energy 431kcal/1800kJ Fat 26.5g Saturated fat 16.2g Carbohydrate 35g Fibre 2.9g.

Lentils Seasoned with Garlic Oil

This dish is popular in southern India, where there are numerous variations. A single vegetable can be added to the lentils, or a combination of two or more. It is traditionally served with steamed rice dumplings or stuffed rice pancakes. The garlic-flavoured lentils are also extremely satisfying with plain boiled rice.

Serves 4–6

120ml/4fl oz/¹⁄₂ cup vegetable oil
2.5ml/¹⁄₂ tsp mustard seeds
2.5ml/¹⁄₂ tsp cumin seeds
2 dried red chillies
1.5ml/¹⁄₄ tsp asafoetida
6–8 curry leaves
2 garlic cloves, crushed, plus 2 sliced
30ml/2 tbsp desiccated (dry unsweetened shredded) coconut
225g/8oz/1 cup red lentils, washed and drained
10ml/2 tsp sambhar masala or other curry powder
2.5ml/¹⁄₂ tsp ground turmeric
450ml/³⁄₄ pint/scant 2 cups water
450g/1lb mixed vegetables, such as okra, courgettes (zucchini), aubergine (eggplant), cauliflower, shallots and (bell) peppers, chopped
60ml/4 tbsp tamarind juice
4 firm tomatoes, quartered
a few coriander (cilantro) leaves, chopped

1 Heat half the oil in a karahi, wok, or large pan, and stir-fry the next seven ingredients until the coconut begins to brown.

2 Stir in the prepared red lentils with the masala and turmeric. Stir-fry for 2–3 minutes and add the water. Bring to the boil and reduce the heat to low.

3 Cover the pan and leave to simmer for 25–30 minutes, or until the lentils are mushy. Add the chopped mixed vegetables, tamarind juice and tomato quarters. Cook until the vegetables are just tender.

4 Heat the remaining oil in a small pan over a low heat, and fry the garlic slices until golden. Stir in the fresh coriander leaves, then pour over the lentils and vegetables. Mix together at the table before serving.

Energy 477kcal/1994kJ Fat 28.7g Saturated fat 7.1g Carbohydrate 38.6g Fibre 6.8g.

Lentils & Rice

Here, lentils are cooked with whole and ground spices, potato, rice and onion to produce a tasty and nutritious meal.

Serves 4

150g/5oz/¾ cup tuvar dhal or red split lentils
115g/4oz/½ cup basmati rice
1 large potato
1 large onion
30ml/2 tbsp oil
4 whole cloves
1.5ml/¼ tsp cumin seeds
1.5ml/¼ tsp ground turmeric
10ml/2 tsp salt
300ml/½ pint/1¼ cups water

1 Wash the tuvar dhal or red split lentils and rice in several changes of cold water. Put into a bowl and cover with water. Leave to soak for 15 minutes, then transfer to a strainer and drain well.

2 Peel the potato, then cut it into 2.5cm/1in chunks. Using a sharp knife, thinly slice the onion and set aside for later.

3 Heat the oil in a heavy pan and fry the cloves and cumin seeds for 2 minutes until the seeds are beginning to splutter.

4 Add the onion and potato chunks and fry for 5 minutes. Add the lentils, rice, turmeric and salt and fry for a further 3 minutes.

5 Add the water. Bring to the boil, cover and simmer gently for 15–20 minutes until all the water has been absorbed and the potato chunks are tender. Leave to stand, covered, for about 10 minutes before serving.

> **Cook's Tip**
> *Red split lentils are widely available in most supermarkets. Before cooking they are salmon-coloured and they turn a pale, dull yellow during cooking. They have a mild, pleasant, nutty flavour. Soaking them in water speeds up the cooking process but isn't strictly necessary.*

Energy 332kcal/1396kJ; Fat 6.7g; Saturated fat 0.76g; Carbohydrate 58.6g; Fibre 3.4g.

Spinach Dhal

Many different types of dhal are eaten in India and each region has its own speciality. This is a delicious, lightly spiced dish with a mild nutty flavour from the yellow lentils, which combine well with the spinach.

Serves 4

175g/6oz/1 cup chana dhal or yellow split peas
175ml/6fl oz/¾ cup water
15ml/1 tbsp oil
1.5ml/¼ tsp black mustard seeds
1 onion, thinly sliced
2 garlic cloves, crushed
2.5cm/1in piece fresh root ginger, grated
1 fresh red chilli, finely chopped
275g/10oz frozen spinach, thawed
1.5ml/¼ tsp chilli powder
2.5ml/½ tsp ground coriander
2.5ml/½ tsp garam masala
2.5ml/½ tsp salt

1 Wash the chana dhal or split peas in several changes of cold water. Put into a bowl and cover with plenty of water. Leave to soak for 30 minutes.

2 Drain the pulses and put them in a large pan with the water. Bring to the boil, cover and simmer for 20–25 minutes, or until they are soft.

3 Meanwhile, heat the oil in a large, heavy pan and fry the mustard seeds for 2 minutes until they begin to splutter.

4 Add the onion, garlic, ginger and chilli and fry for 5–6 minutes until softened but not coloured.

5 Add the spinach and cook for 10 minutes or until the spinach is dry and the liquid has been absorbed. Stir in the remaining spices and salt, and cook for 2–3 minutes.

6 Drain the split peas, add them to the spinach mixture and cook for about 5 minutes. Transfer to a warmed serving dish and serve immediately.

Energy 183kcal/778kJ Fat 2g Saturated fat 0.44g Carbohydrate 30.3g Fibre 4.9g.

South Indian Lentils & Vegetables

Pulses are perfect for easy, inexpensive meals. Choose a selection of your favourite vegetables, such as potato, cauliflower, carrots and beans for this tasty dish.

Serves 4–6

60ml/4 tbsp vegetable oil
2.5ml/½ tsp mustard seeds
2.5ml/½ tsp cumin seeds
2 dried red chillies
1.5ml/¼ tsp asafoetida
6–8 curry leaves
2 garlic cloves, crushed
30ml/2 tbsp desiccated (dry unsweetened shredded) coconut

225g/8oz/1 cup masoor dhal or red split lentils
10ml/2 tsp sambhar masala or garam masala
2.5ml/½ tsp ground turmeric
450g/1lb mixed vegetables, in bitesize pieces
60ml/4 tbsp tamarind juice
4 firm tomatoes, quartered
60ml/4 tbsp vegetable oil
2 garlic cloves, finely sliced
handful fresh coriander (cilantro), chopped

1 Heat the oil in a heavy pan. Fry the mustard seeds, cumin seeds, dried red chillies, asafoetida, curry leaves, crushed garlic and desiccated coconut until the coconut browns.

2 Mix in the masoor dhal or red split lentils, sambhar masala and ground turmeric. Stir in 450ml/¾ pint/scant 2 cups water.

3 Simmer the mixture until the lentils are mushy. Add the mixed vegetables, tamarind juice and tomatoes. Cook so that the vegetables are crunchy.

4 In the oil, fry the garlic slices and fresh coriander. Pour over the lentils and vegetables. Mix at the table before serving.

> **Cook's Tip**
> Courgettes (zucchini), aubergines (eggplants), (bell) peppers, mangetouts (snow peas) and broccoli would also taste wonderful in this curry.

Energy 459kcal/1917kJ; Fat 28.1g; Saturated fat 7g; Carbohydrate 37.3g; Fibre 5.8g.

Rice Layered with Bengal Gram

This rice and lentil dish is served with a gourd curry, or palida, which is prominently flavoured with fenugreek and soured with dried mangosteen.

Serves 4–6

175g/6oz/⅔ cup Bengal gram or lentils of your choice
600ml/1 pint/2½ cups water
2.5ml/½ tsp ground turmeric
50g/2oz deep-fried onions, crushed
45ml/3 tbsp green masala paste
a few fresh mint and coriander (cilantro) leaves, chopped
350g/12oz/1¾ cups basmati rice, cooked
30ml/2 tbsp ghee
salt

For the curry

60ml/4 tbsp vegetable oil
1.5ml/¼ tsp fenugreek seeds
15g/½oz dried fenugreek leaves
2 garlic cloves, crushed
5ml/1 tsp ground coriander
5ml/1 tsp cumin seeds
5ml/1 tsp chilli powder
60ml/4 tbsp gram flour mixed with 60ml/4 tbsp water
450g/1lb bottle gourd, peeled, pith and seeds removed and cut into bitesize pieces, or marrow (large zucchini) or firm courgettes (zucchini) prepared in the same way
175ml/6fl oz/¾ cup tomato juice
6 dried mangosteen (kokum), or juice of 3 lemons
salt

1 For the rice, boil the Bengal gram in the water with the turmeric until the grains are soft. Drain and reserve the water for the curry. Toss the Bengal gram gently with the deep-fried onions, green masala paste, mint and coriander. Add salt to taste.

2 Grease a heavy pan and place a layer of rice in the bottom. Add the bengal gram mixture and another layer of the remaining rice. Place small knobs (pats) of ghee on top, sprinkle with a little water and heat gently until steam rises from the mixture.

3 To make the curry, heat the oil in a pan and fry the fenugreek seeds and leaves and the garlic until the garlic turns golden brown. Mix the ground coriander, cumin and chilli powder to a paste with a little water. Add to the pan and simmer until all the water has evaporated. Add the gram-flour paste, gourd and the tomato juice. Add the mangosteen and salt. Cook until the gourd is soft. Serve hot.

Energy 536kcal/2250kJ; Fat 14g; Saturated fat 1.8g; Carbohydrate 82.3g; Fibre 4.9g.

Lentil Dhal with Roasted Garlic & Whole Spices

This spicy lentil dhal makes a sustaining and comforting meal when served with rice or Indian breads and any dry-spiced dish, particularly a cauliflower or potato dish. The spicy garnish offers a contrast in texture and flavour.

Serves 4–6

40g/1½oz/3 tbsp butter or
  ghee
1 onion, chopped
2 fresh green chillies, seeded
  and chopped
15ml/1 tbsp chopped fresh
  root ginger
225g/8oz/1 cup yellow or
  red lentils
900ml/1½ pints/3¾ cups water
45ml/3 tbsp roasted garlic purée

5ml/1 tsp ground cumin
5ml/1 tsp ground coriander
200g/7oz tomatoes, peeled
  and diced
a little lemon juice
salt and ground black pepper
30–45ml/2–3 tbsp coriander
  (cilantro) sprigs, to garnish

For the spicy garnish

30ml/2 tbsp groundnut
  (peanut) oil
4 or 5 shallots, sliced
2 garlic cloves, thinly sliced
15g/½oz/1 tbsp butter or
  ghee
5ml/1 tsp cumin seeds
5ml/1 tsp mustard seeds
3 or 4 small dried red chillies
8–10 fresh curry leaves

1 First begin the spicy garnish. Heat the oil in a large, heavy pan. Add the shallots and fry them over a medium heat, stirring occasionally, until they are crisp and browned. Add the garlic and cook, stirring frequently, for a moment or two until the garlic colours slightly. Use a slotted spoon to remove the mixture from the pan and set it aside in a bowl.

2 Melt the butter or ghee in the pan and cook the onion, chillies and ginger for 10 minutes, until golden. Stir in the lentils and water, then bring to the boil, reduce the heat and part-cover the pan. Simmer, stirring occasionally, for 50–60 minutes, until similar to a very thick soup.

3 Stir in the roasted garlic purée, cumin and ground coriander, then season with salt and pepper to taste. Cook for a further 10–15 minutes, uncovered, stirring frequently. Stir in the tomatoes and then adjust the seasoning, adding a little lemon juice to taste if necessary.

4 Finish the spicy garnish. Melt the butter or ghee in a frying pan. Add the cumin and mustard seeds and fry until the mustard seeds pop. Stir in the chillies, curry leaves and the shallot mixture, then immediately swirl the mixture into the cooked dhal. Garnish with coriander and serve.

> **Cook's Tip**
> *Ghee is a type of clarified butter that has had all the milk solids removed by heating. Because the milk solids have been removed, ghee has a high smoking point and can therefore be cooked at higher temperatures than ordinary butter.*

Energy 340kcal/1424kJ; Fat 16.3g; Saturated fat 7.5g; Carbohydrate 36.3g; Fibre 3.8g.

Bengal Gram & Bottle Gourd Curry

Tamarind gives this lentil and vegetable dish a lemony flavour. Rice or Indian bread is all you need to go with it.

Serves 4–6

450g/1lb bottle gourd, marrow
  (large zucchini)
175g/6oz/⅔ cup Bengal gram
scant 60ml/4 tbsp vegetable oil
2 fresh green chillies, chopped
1 onion, chopped
2 garlic cloves, crushed

5cm/2in piece fresh root
  ginger, crushed
6–8 curry leaves
5ml/1 tsp chilli powder
5ml/1 tsp ground turmeric
60ml/4 tbsp tamarind juice
2 tomatoes, chopped
chopped fresh coriander
  (cilantro)
salt

1 Peel the bottle gourd making sure that the pith is removed. Slice the gourd flesh thickly.

2 Put the Bengal gram in a pan with 450ml/¾ pint/scant 2 cups water, cook the lentils in the water until the grains are tender but not mushy. Set aside, without draining away any of the excess water.

3 Heat the vegetable oil in a large pan and fry the chopped green chillies and onion, crushed garlic, crushed ginger, curry leaves, chilli powder and ground turmeric. Add salt to taste.

4 Add the gourd slices and cook until soft.

5 Add the lentils to the gourd mixture in the pan and any water remaining in the pan. Bring to the boil. Stir in the tamarind juice, chopped tomatoes and fresh chopped coriander.

6 Simmer gently until the gourd is cooked. Serve hot with rice.

Energy 280kcal/1173kJ; Fat 12.2g; Saturated fat 1.6g; Carbohydrate 31.1g; Fibre 4.2g.

Cucumber Curry

Served hot, this unusual curry is good with main-course vegetable dishes, and can also be served cold.

Serves 4–6

120ml/4fl oz/½ cup water
115g/4oz creamed coconut
  (120ml/4fl oz/½ cup coconut
  cream)
2.5ml/½ tsp ground turmeric
5ml/1 tsp sugar
1 large cucumber, cut into
  small pieces

1 large red (bell) pepper,
  cut into small pieces
50g/2oz/½ cup salted peanuts,
  crushed
60ml/4 tbsp vegetable oil
2 dried red chillies
5ml/1 tsp cumin seeds
5ml/1 tsp mustard
  seeds
4–6 curry leaves
4 garlic cloves, crushed
salt
a few whole salted peanuts,
  to garnish

1 Bring the water to the boil in a heavy pan and add the creamed coconut, turmeric, sugar and salt. Simmer until the coconut dissolves and the mixture becomes a smooth, thick sauce.

2 Add the cucumber, red pepper and crushed peanuts and simmer for about 5 minutes. Transfer to a heatproof serving dish and keep hot.

3 Heat the oil in a karahi, wok or frying pan. Fry the chillies and cumin with the mustard seeds until they start to pop.

4 Reduce the heat, add the curry leaves and garlic and fry for 2 minutes. Pour over the cucumber mixture and stir well. Garnish with whole peanuts and serve hot.

Cook's Tip
The mustard seeds used extensively in Indian cooking are black and not yellow (which are ground and used to prepare English mustard). They are always fried to release their sweet aroma and flavour.

Spicy Cabbage

Another spicy twist on a Western favourite. This nutritious side dish is a great way to jazz up the flavour of cabbage for those not usually keen on the vegetable. Note the colourful variations.

Serves 4

225g/8oz/2½ cups shredded
  cabbage
1 small onion, sliced

2 medium carrots, grated
50g/2oz/¼ cup ghee or
  butter
2.5ml/½ tsp white cumin
  seeds
3–8 dried red chillies, to taste
2.5ml/½ tsp salt
30ml/2 tbsp lemon juice

1 Use a mandolin, if you have one, to shred the cabbage finely. Alternatively, use a sharp knife to slice through the layers of the cabbage.

2 Slice the onion and grate the carrots coarsely.

3 Melt the ghee or butter in a medium pan and fry the cumin seeds and dried chillies for about 30 seconds.

4 Add the onion and fry for about 2 minutes.

5 Add the cabbage and carrots and stir-fry for a further 5 minutes or until the cabbage is soft.

6 Finally, stir in the salt and lemon juice and serve immediately.

Variations
You will get a different appearance as well as flavour if you use different kinds of cabbage for this recipe. White cabbage has a delicate taste, whereas Savoy cabbage and spring greens (collards) have a fuller flavour. You could also try red cabbage and use a red onion as well for a colourful alternative.

Energy 385kcal/1588kJ; Fat 37.6g; Saturated fat 19.6g; Carbohydrate 6.4g; Fibre 1.7g.

Energy 91kcal/376kJ; Fat 5.5g; Saturated fat 1.27g; Carbohydrate 8.5g; Fibre 2.4g.

Karahi Shredded Cabbage with Mangetouts & Corn

This is one of the best ways to cook cabbage, stir-fried with butter and crushed spices. This side dish makes a wonderful accompaniment to many vegetable dishes.

Serves 4
15ml/1 tbsp corn oil
50g/2oz/¼ cup ghee or butter
2.5ml/½ tsp crushed coriander
  seeds
2.5ml/½ tsp white cumin seeds
6 dried red chillies

1 small Savoy cabbage, shredded
12 mangetouts (snow peas)
3 fresh red chillies, seeded
  and sliced
12 baby corn cobs
salt
25g/1oz/¼ cup flaked (sliced)
  almonds, toasted, and 15ml/
  1 tbsp chopped fresh coriander
  (cilantro), to garnish

1 Heat the oil and butter in a deep round-bottomed frying pan or a karahi and add the crushed coriander seeds, white cumin seeds and dried red chillies.

2 Add the shredded cabbage and mangetouts, and stir-fry for about 5 minutes.

3 Add the sliced fresh red chillies, baby corn and salt, and fry for a further 3 minutes.

4 Garnish with the toasted almonds and fresh coriander and serve hot.

Cook's Tip
This dish is strongly spiced with red chillies, both fresh and dried, but the recipe also works well with fewer chillies if you prefer a milder flavour. If you have large dried red chillies in your store cupboard (pantry) you might want to reduce the quantity to just one.

Energy 184kcal/759kJ; Fat 16.9g; Saturated fat 7.2g; Carbohydrate 4.3g; Fibre 3g.

Curried Cauliflower

In this dish the creamy coconut sauce beautifully complements the flavour of the spiced cauliflower.

Serves 4–6
15ml/1 tbsp gram flour
120ml/4fl oz/½ cup water
5ml/1 tsp chilli powder
15ml/1 tbsp ground coriander
5ml/1 tsp ground cumin
5ml/1 tsp mustard powder
5ml/1 tsp ground turmeric
60ml/4 tbsp vegetable oil
6–8 curry leaves
5ml/1 tsp cumin seeds
1 cauliflower, broken into florets
175ml/6fl oz/¾ cup thick
  coconut milk
juice of 2 lemons
salt
lime wedges, to serve

1 Put the gram flour in a small bowl and stir in enough of the water to make a smooth paste.

2 Add the chilli, coriander, cumin, mustard, turmeric and salt. Add the remaining water and keep mixing to blend all the ingredients well.

3 Heat the oil in a frying pan, and add the curry leaves and cumin seeds. Add the spice paste and simmer for about 5 minutes, stirring frequently. If the sauce has become too thick, add a little hot water.

4 Add the cauliflower florets and the coconut milk. Bring the mixture to the boil and then reduce the heat. Cover with a lid and cook until the cauliflower is tender but still retains a bit of a crunch. (If you like your cauliflower more tender, cook for a little longer.)

5 Add the lemon juice, mix well and serve the curry hot with the wedges of lime to squeeze over.

Variation
This sauce also goes well with broccoli. To create a pretty presentation, use whole miniature vegetables.

Energy 160kcal/663kJ; Fat 12.1g; Saturated fat 1.6g; Carbohydrate 9g; Fibre 2g.

Spiced Aubergine

Chunks of aubergine are coated in a rich sauce and sprinkled with sesame seeds to make an unusual side dish that is quick to cook. This straightforward yet versatile vegetarian dish can be served hot, warm or cold, as the occasion demands.

Serves 4–6
2 aubergines, total weight about 600g/1lb 6oz, cut into large chunks
15ml/1 tbsp salt
5ml/1 tsp chilli powder, or to taste

75–90ml/5–6 tbsp sunflower oil
15ml/1 tbsp rice wine or medium-dry sherry
100ml/3½fl oz/scant ½ cup water
75ml/5 tbsp chilli bean sauce (see Cook's Tip)
salt and ground black pepper
a few toasted sesame seeds, to garnish

1 Place the aubergine chunks on a plate, sprinkle them with the salt and leave to stand for 15–20 minutes. Rinse well, drain and dry thoroughly on kitchen paper. Toss the aubergine cubes in the chilli powder.

2 Heat a wok and add the oil. When the oil is hot, add the aubergine chunks, with the rice wine or sherry. Stir constantly until the aubergine chunks start to turn a little brown. Stir in the water, cover the wok and steam for 2–3 minutes. Add the chilli bean sauce and cook for 2 minutes. Season to taste, then spoon on to a serving dish, sprinkle with sesame seeds and serve.

> **Cook's Tip**
> If you can't get hold of chilli bean sauce, use 15–30ml/ 1–2 tbsp chilli paste mixed with 2 crushed garlic cloves, 15ml/1 tbsp each dark soy sauce and rice vinegar, and 10ml/2 tsp light soy sauce.

Energy 193kcal/798kJ; Fat 17.1g; Saturated fat 2.1g; Carbohydrate 8.7g; Fibre 3.2g.

Carrot & Cauliflower Stir-fry

Slicing the carrots into thin batons helps them cook quickly. This dish has a crunchy texture and uses only a few whole spices.

Serves 4
2 large carrots
1 small cauliflower
15ml/1 tbsp oil
1 bay leaf

2 cloves
1 small cinnamon stick
2 cardamom pods
3 black peppercorns
5ml/1 tsp salt
50g/2oz/½ cup frozen peas, thawed
10ml/2 tsp lemon juice
15ml/1 tbsp chopped fresh coriander (cilantro), plus fresh leaves to garnish

1 Cut the carrots into thin batons about 2.5cm/1in long. Separate the cauliflower into small florets.

2 Heat the oil in a karahi, wok or heavy pan and add the bay leaf, cloves, cinnamon stick, cardamom pods and peppercorns. Quickly stir-fry over a medium heat for 30–35 seconds, then add the salt.

3 Next add the carrot batons and cauliflower florets and continue to stir-fry for 3–5 minutes.

4 Add the peas, lemon juice and chopped coriander and cook for a further 4–5 minutes. Serve garnished with the whole coriander leaves.

> **Variation**
> Substitute broccoli or sliced courgette (zucchini) for the cauliflower, if you like.

> **Cook's Tip**
> As both carrots and cauliflower can be eaten raw, they need only minimal cooking or they will lose their crunchy texture.

Energy 84kcal/349kJ; Fat 3.75g; Saturated fat 0.6g; Carbohydrate 9.05g; Fibre 3.67g.

Cauliflower & Potato Curry

Potatoes and cauliflower make a wonderful combination for a curry, and a substantial side dish. Here they are combined with the mild flavours of cumin, coriander and turmeric with just enough chilli to give the dish that little extra punch.

Serves 4
450g/1lb potatoes, cut into
  2.5cm/1in chunks
30ml/2 tbsp oil
5ml/1 tsp cumin seeds
1 fresh green chilli, finely chopped
450g/1lb cauliflower, broken
  into florets
5ml/1 tsp ground coriander
5ml/1 tsp ground cumin
1.5ml/¼ tsp chilli powder
2.5ml/½ tsp ground turmeric
2.5ml/½ tsp salt
chopped fresh coriander (cilantro),
  to garnish
tomato and onion salad and
  pickle, to serve

1 Par-cook the potatoes in a large pan of boiling water for about 10 minutes. Drain well and set aside.

2 Heat the oil in a large, heavy pan. Add the cumin seeds and fry them for 2 minutes until they begin to splutter. Add the chilli and fry for a further 1 minute.

3 Add the cauliflower florets and fry, stirring, for 5 minutes.

4 Add the potatoes and the ground spices and salt and cook for a further 7–10 minutes, or until both the vegetables are tender. Garnish with fresh coriander and serve with tomato and onion salad and pickle.

> **Variation**
> Use sweet potatoes instead of ordinary potatoes for a curry with a sweeter flavour.

Energy 189kcal/791kJ; Fat 7.4g; Saturated fat 0.77g; Carbohydrate 24.6g; Fibre 3.5g.

Spicy Potatoes & Cauliflower

This dish is simplicity itself to make and can be eaten with Indian breads or rice, a raita such as cucumber and yogurt, and a fresh mint relish.

Serves 2
225g/8oz potatoes
75ml/5 tbsp groundnut
  (peanut) oil
5ml/1 tsp ground cumin
5ml/1 tsp ground coriander
1.5ml/¼ tsp ground turmeric
1.5ml/¼ tsp cayenne pepper
1 fresh green chilli, seeded
  and finely chopped
1 medium cauliflower, broken
  into small florets
5ml/1 tsp cumin seeds
2 garlic cloves, cut into
  shreds
15–30ml/1–2 tbsp fresh
  coriander (cilantro),
  finely chopped
salt

1 Cook the potatoes in their skins in boiling salted water for about 20 minutes, until just tender. Drain and leave to cool. When cool enough to handle, peel and cut into 2.5cm/1in cubes.

2 Heat 45ml/3 tbsp of the oil in a frying pan or wok. When hot, add the ground cumin, coriander, turmeric, cayenne pepper and chilli. Let the spices sizzle for a few seconds.

3 Add the cauliflower and about 60ml/4 tbsp water. Cook over medium heat, stirring continuously, for 6–8 minutes. Add the potatoes and stir-fry for 2–3 minutes. Season with salt, then remove from the heat.

4 Heat the remaining oil in a small frying pan. When hot, add the cumin seeds and garlic, and cook until lightly browned. Pour the mixture over the vegetables. Sprinkle with the chopped coriander and serve at once.

> **Cook's Tip**
> Divide the cauliflower into small florets so that it will cook evenly and quickly.

Energy 409kcal/1698kJ; Fat 29.7g; Saturated fat 3.8g; Carbohydrate 26.6g; Fibre 5.4g.

Potatoes in Tomato Sauce

This delicious curry makes an excellent accompaniment to almost any other savoury dish, but goes particularly well with Balti dishes. Served with rice, it could also make a great vegetarian main course.

Serves 4
10ml/2 tsp oil
1.5ml/¼ tsp onion seeds
4 curry leaves
2 medium onions, diced
400g/14oz can tomatoes
5ml/1 tsp ground cumin
7.5ml/1½ tsp ground coriander
5ml/1 tsp chilli powder
5ml/1 tsp grated fresh root ginger
5ml/1 tsp crushed garlic
1.5ml/¼ tsp ground turmeric
5ml/1 tsp salt
15ml/1 tbsp lemon juice
15ml/1 tbsp chopped fresh
   coriander (cilantro)
2 medium potatoes, diced

1 Heat the oil in a karahi, wok or heavy pan and add the onion seeds, curry leaves and diced onions. Fry over a medium heat for a few minutes, stirring occasionally and being careful not to burn the onions.

2 Meanwhile, place the canned tomatoes in a bowl and add the ground cumin and coriander, chilli powder, ginger, garlic, turmeric, salt, lemon juice and fresh coriander. Mix the ingredients together until well blended.

3 Pour this mixture into the pan and stir for about 1 minute to mix thoroughly with the onions.

4 Finally, add the diced potatoes, cover the pan and cook gently for 7–10 minutes over low heat. Check that the potatoes are properly cooked through, then serve.

> **Variations**
> This curry is also delicious if you add a few cauliflower or broccoli florets with the potatoes, or if you substitute diced parsnips for the potatoes. To emphasize the tomato flavour, stir in 15ml/1 tbsp tomato purée (paste).

Potatoes in Red Sauce

This is a lightly spiced dish, perfect for children or those who like mild curries.

Serves 4–6
450g/1lb small new potatoes
7.5ml/1½ tsp coriander
   seeds
7.5ml/1½ tsp cumin seeds
4 garlic cloves
90ml/6 tbsp vegetable oil
45ml/3 tbsp thick tamarind
   juice (see Cook's Tip)
60ml/4 tbsp tomato purée
   (paste)
4 curry leaves
salt
5ml/1 tsp granulated sugar
coriander (cilantro) sprig,
   to garnish

1 Boil the potatoes until they are fully cooked but still retain their shape. To test, insert a thin sharp knife into the potatoes. It should come out clean when the potatoes are fully cooked. Drain well.

2 Grind the coriander seeds with the cumin seeds and garlic to a coarse paste using a mortar and pestle or food processor.

3 Heat the oil in a karahi, wok or frying pan. Fry the paste, tamarind juice, tomato purée, curry leaves, salt and sugar until the oil separates.

4 Add the potatoes and stir to coat them in the spicy tomato mixture. Reduce the heat, cover the pan and simmer for about 5 minutes. Garnish and serve.

> **Cook's Tip**
> You can buy tamarind concentrate or break off a piece of tamarind slab equivalent to 15ml/1 tbsp. Soak in 150ml/ ¼ pint/⅔ cup hot water for 10 minutes. Mash the tamarind into a paste and pass it through a sieve (strainer). The fine pulp and juice will go through, leaving behind the fibrous husk. Strain the juice. Tamarind pods have a long shelf life and they require soaking to release their juice.

Energy 119kcal/502kJ; Fat 2.27g; Saturated fat 0.24g; Carbohydrate 22.91g; Fibre 2.88g.

Energy 231kcal/962kJ; Fat 16.8g; Saturated fat 2.1g; Carbohydrate 19.2g; Fibre 1.1g.

Bombay Potatoes

This authentic dish belongs to the Gujarati, a totally vegetarian sect and the largest population group in the city of Mumbai.

Serves 4–6
2 onions
2 fresh green chillies
50g/2oz/2 cups fresh coriander (cilantro)
450g/1lb new potatoes
5ml/1 tsp turmeric
60ml/4 tbsp vegetable oil
2 dried red chillies
6–8 curry leaves
1.5ml/¼ tsp asafoetida
2.5ml/½ tsp each cumin, mustard, onion, fennel and nigella seeds
lemon juice, to taste
salt

1 Chop the onions and chillies finely, and coarsely chop the coriander.

2 Scrub the potatoes under cold running water and cut them into small pieces.

3 Boil the potatoes in water with a little salt and 2.5ml/½ tsp of the turmeric for 10–15 minutes, or until tender. Drain the potatoes well then mash them and set aside.

4 Heat the oil in a frying pan and fry the dried chillies and curry leaves until the chillies are nearly burnt.

5 Add the sliced onions, green chillies, fresh coriander and remaining turmeric to the pan, add the asafoetida, cumin, mustard, onion, fennel and nigella seeds. Cook, stirring occasionally, until the onions are soft.

6 Fold in the potatoes and add a few drops of water. Cook over a low heat for about 10 minutes, stirring well to ensure the spices are evenly mixed.

7 Add lemon juice to taste, and serve immediately.

Energy 207kcal/865kJ; Fat 11.6g; Saturated fat 1.4g; Carbohydrate 24.3g; Fibre 2.2g.

Spinach & Potatoes & Red Chillies

India is blessed with over 18 varieties of spinach. If you have access to an Indian or Chinese grocer, look out for some of the more unusual varieties.

Serves 4–6
225g/8oz potatoes
60ml/4 tbsp vegetable oil
2.5cm/1in piece fresh root ginger, crushed
4 garlic cloves, crushed
1 onion, chopped
2 fresh green chillies, chopped
2 dried red chillies, chopped
5ml/1 tsp cumin seeds
225g/8oz fresh spinach, trimmed, washed and chopped, or 225g/8oz frozen spinach, thawed and drained
salt
2 firm tomatoes, roughly chopped, to garnish

1 Wash the potatoes and cut into quarters. If using small new potatoes, leave them whole. Heat the oil in a frying pan and fry the potatoes until brown on all sides. Remove and put aside.

2 Remove the excess oil, leaving about 15ml/1 tbsp in the pan. Fry the ginger, garlic, onion, green chillies, dried red chillies and cumin seeds until the onion is golden brown.

3 Add the potatoes and salt, and stir well. Cover the pan and cook over a medium heat, stirring occasionally, until the potatoes are tender when pierced with a sharp knife.

4 Add the spinach and stir well. Using two wooden spoons or spatulas, toss the mixture over the heat until the spinach is tender and all the excess fluid has evaporated.

5 Spoon into a heated serving dish or on to individual plates and garnish with the chopped tomatoes. Serve hot.

> **Variation**
> This recipe also tastes very good if you substitute sweet potatoes for ordinary potatoes. Slice them just before cooking, or they may discolour.

Energy 177kcal/734kJ; Fat 11.8g; Saturated fat 1.4g; Carbohydrate 15g; Fibre 2.9g.

Fiery Spiced Potatoes

The quantity of red chillies used here may be too fiery for some palates. For a milder version, seed the chillies, use fewer, or substitute them with a roughly chopped sweet red pepper instead.

Serves 4

12–14 baby new potatoes, peeled and halved
15ml/1 tbsp oil
2.5ml/½ tsp crushed dried red chillies
2.5ml/½ tsp cumin seeds
2.5ml/½ tsp fennel seeds
2.5ml/½ tsp crushed coriander seeds
1 medium onion, sliced
3 or 4 fresh red chillies, chopped
15ml/1 tbsp chopped fresh coriander (cilantro)
salt

1 Boil the potatoes in a pan of salted water until just cooked but still firm. Remove from the heat and drain off the water.

2 In a karahi, wok or deep pan, heat the oil quickly over high heat, then turn down the heat to medium. Add the crushed chillies, cumin, fennel and coriander seeds and a little salt and quickly stir-fry for about 30–40 seconds.

3 Add the onion and fry gently until golden brown. Then add the new potatoes, fresh red chillies and fresh coriander.

4 Cover and cook for 5–7 minutes over a very low heat. Serve hot.

Cook's Tip
Baby new potatoes have a wonderful flavour and texture, which are absolutely perfect for this dish. If you want to try older potatoes, choose ones that retain their shape well and cut them into large chunks. Watch them carefully so that they do not overcook and fall apart.

Energy 122kcal/513kJ; Fat 3.5g; Saturated fat 0.37g; Carbohydrate 21.2g; Fibre 1.5g.

Spiced Potatoes & Carrots Parisienne

Ready-prepared "parisienne" vegetables have recently become available in many supermarkets. These are simply root vegetables that have been peeled and cut into perfectly spherical shapes. This dish looks very fresh and appetizing and is delicious. If you can't locate "parisienne" vegetables, you can simply dice the potatoes and carrots yourself, or cut them into batons.

Serves 4

175g/6oz carrots parisienne
175g/6oz potatoes parisienne
115g/4oz green beans, sliced
75g/3oz/6 tbsp butter
15ml/1 tbsp vegetable oil
1.5ml/¼ tsp onion seeds
1.5ml/¼ tsp fenugreek seeds
4 dried red chillies
2.5ml/½ tsp mustard seeds
6 curry leaves
1 medium onion, sliced
5ml/1 tsp salt
4 garlic cloves, sliced
4 fresh red chillies
15ml/1 tbsp chopped fresh coriander (cilantro)
15ml/1 tbsp chopped fresh mint, plus 1 mint sprig to garnish

1 Drop the carrots, potatoes and green beans into a pan of boiling water, and cook for about 7 minutes, or until they are just tender but not overcooked. Drain in a colander, then refresh under cold water to arrest the cooking process. Drain again and set to one side.

2 Heat the butter and oil in a deep frying pan or a large karahi and add the onion seeds, fenugreek seeds, dried red chillies, mustard seeds and curry leaves. When these have sizzled for a few seconds, add the onion and fry for 3–5 minutes, stirring the mixture occasionally.

3 Add the salt, garlic and fresh chillies, followed by the cooked vegetables, and stir gently for about 5 minutes, over a medium heat.

4 Add the fresh coriander and mint, and serve hot, garnished with a sprig of mint.

Energy 232kcal/961kJ; Fat 18.6g; Saturated fat 10.2g; Carbohydrate 15g; Fibre 2.7g.

Masala Mashed Potatoes

This delightfully simple variation on the popular Western side dish can be used as an accompaniment to just about any main course dish, not just Indian food. There are easily obtainable alternatives to mango powder if you cannot get hold of any (see Cook's Tip).

Serves 4

3 medium potatoes
15ml/1 tbsp chopped fresh mint and coriander (cilantro), mixed
5ml/1 tsp mango powder (amchur)
5ml/1 tsp salt
5ml/1 tsp crushed black peppercorns
1 fresh red chilli, chopped
1 fresh green chilli, chopped
50g/2oz/¼ cup butter

1 Boil the potatoes until soft and then mash them down using a masher or potato ricer.

2 Stir the remaining ingredients together in a small bowl.

3 Stir the spice mixture into the mashed potatoes. Mix together thoroughly with a fork and serve warm as an accompaniment.

Cook's Tip
Mango powder, also known as amchur, is the unripe green fruit of the mango tree ground to a powder. The sour mangoes are sliced and dried in the sun, turning a light brown, before they are ground. Mango powder adds a fruity sharpness and a slightly resinous bouquet to a dish. It is widely used with vegetables and is usually added towards the end of the cooking time. If mango powder is unavailable, the nearest substitute is lemon or lime juice, in double or treble quantity.

Energy 100kcal/416kJ; Fat 5.3g; Saturated fat 1.25g; Carbohydrate 11.4g; Fibre 0.8g.

Potatoes in Yogurt Sauce

It is nice to use tiny new potatoes with the skins on for this recipe. The yogurt adds a tangy flavour to this fairly spicy dish, which is delicious served with plain or wholemeal chapatis.

Serves 4

small bunch fresh coriander (cilantro)
12 new potatoes, halved
275g/10oz/1¼ cups natural (plain) low-fat yogurt
300ml/½ pint/1¼ cups water
1.5ml/¼ tsp ground turmeric
5ml/1 tsp chilli powder
5ml/1 tsp ground coriander
2.5ml/½ tsp ground cumin
5ml/1 tsp soft brown sugar
1.5ml/¼ tsp salt
15ml/1 tbsp oil
5ml/1 tsp cumin seeds
2 green chillies, sliced

1 Cut off the roots and any thick stalks from the coriander and chop the leaves finely. Set aside.

2 Boil the potatoes in salted water with their skins on until they are just tender, then drain and set aside.

3 Mix together the yogurt, water, turmeric, chilli powder, ground coriander, ground cumin, sugar and salt in a bowl. Set aside.

4 Heat the oil in a medium, heavy pan and stir in the cumin seeds. Fry for 1 minute.

5 Reduce the heat, stir in the spicy yogurt mixture and cook for about 3 minutes over medium heat.

6 Add the chopped fresh coriander, green chillies and cooked potatoes. Blend everything together and cook for a further 5–7 minutes, stirring from time to time. Serve hot.

Cook's Tip
If new potatoes are unavailable, use 450g/1lb ordinary waxy potatoes instead. Peel them and cut into large chunks, then cook as described above.

Energy 169kcal/712kJ; Fat 4.3g; Saturated fat 0.78g; Carbohydrate 27.6g; Fibre 1.2g.

Potatoes in Chilli Tamarind Sauce

In this favourite potato dish from the state of Karnataka, the combination of chilli and tamarind awakens the taste buds immediately. This version adapts the traditional recipe slightly, to reduce the customary pungency and enhance the fiery appearance of this delicious combination.

Serves 4–6
450g/1lb small new potatoes, washed and dried
25g/1oz whole dried red chillies, preferably Kashmiri
7.5ml/1½ tsp cumin seeds
4 garlic cloves, chopped
90ml/6 tbsp vegetable oil
60ml/4 tbsp thick tamarind juice
30ml/2 tbsp tomato purée (paste)
4 curry leaves
5ml/1 tsp granulated sugar
1.5ml/¼ tsp asafoetida
salt
coriander (cilantro) sprigs and lemon wedges, to garnish

1 Boil the new potatoes until they are fully cooked, ensuring they do not break. To test, insert a thin sharp knife into the potatoes. It should come out clean when they are fully cooked. Drain and cool the potatoes in iced water to prevent them from cooking further.

2 Soak the chillies for 5 minutes in warm water. Drain and grind with the cumin seeds and garlic to a coarse paste, either using a mortar and pestle or in a food processor.

3 Heat the oil and fry the paste, tamarind juice, tomato purée, curry leaves, sugar, asafoetida and salt until the oil can be seen to have separated from the spice paste.

4 Add the potatoes and stir to coat. Reduce the heat, cover and simmer for 5 minutes. Garnish and serve.

Variation
Chunks of large potatoes can be used as an alternative to new potatoes. Alternatively, try this dish with sweet potatoes. The spicy sweet-and-sour taste works very well in this variation.

Potatoes with Roasted Poppy Seeds

Poppy seeds are used in Indian cooking as thickening agents, and to lend a nutty taste to sauces.

Serves 4
45ml/3 tbsp white poppy seeds
45–60ml/3–4 tbsp vegetable oil
675g/1½lb potatoes, peeled and cut into 1cm/½in cubes
2.5ml/½ tsp black mustard seeds
2.5ml/½ tsp onion seeds
2.5ml/½ tsp cumin seeds
2.5ml/½ tsp fennel seeds
1 or 2 dried red chillies, chopped or broken into small pieces
2.5ml/½ tsp ground turmeric
2.5ml/½ tsp salt
150ml/¼ pint/⅔ cup warm water
fresh coriander (cilantro) sprigs, to garnish
pooris and natural (plain) yogurt, to serve

1 Preheat a karahi, wok or large pan over a medium setting. When the pan is hot, reduce the heat slightly and add the poppy seeds. Stir them around in the pan until they are just a shade darker. Remove from the pan and leave to cool.

2 In the pan, heat the vegetable oil over a medium heat and fry the cubes of potato until they are light brown. Remove them with a slotted spoon and drain on kitchen paper.

3 To the same oil, add the mustard seeds. As soon as they begin to pop, add the onion, cumin and fennel seeds and the chillies. Let the chillies blacken, but remove them from the pan before they burn.

4 Stir in the turmeric and follow quickly with the fried potatoes and salt. Stir well and add the warm water. Cover the pan with the lid and reduce the heat to low. Cook for 8–10 minutes, or until the potatoes are tender.

5 Grind the cooled poppy seeds in a mortar and pestle or spice grinder. Stir the ground seeds into the potatoes. It should form a thick paste which should cling to the potatoes. If there is too much liquid, continue to stir over a medium heat until you have the right consistency. Transfer to a serving dish. Garnish with coriander and serve with pooris and natural yogurt.

Energy 227kcal/945kJ; Fat 16.8g; Saturated fat 2.1g; Carbohydrate 18.1g; Fibre 1.1g.

Energy 201kcal/842kJ; Fat 13.5g; Saturated fat 1.6g; Carbohydrate 29g; Fibre 2.2g.

Spinach with Mushrooms

A tasty vegetable that is often overlooked, spinach is highly nutritious. Cooked in this way it tastes wonderful. Serve with chapatis.

Serves 4

450g/1lb fresh or frozen
  spinach, thawed
30ml/2 tbsp oil
2 medium onions, diced
6–8 curry leaves
1.5ml/¼ tsp onion seeds
5ml/1 tsp crushed garlic
5ml/1 tsp grated fresh root ginger
5ml/1 tsp chilli powder
5ml/1 tsp salt
7.5ml/1½ tsp ground coriander
1 large red (bell) pepper, seeded
  and sliced
115g/4oz/1½ cups mushrooms,
  roughly chopped
225g/8oz/1 cup low-fat fromage
  frais or ricotta cheese
30ml/2 tbsp fresh coriander
  (cilantro) leaves

1 If using fresh spinach, blanch it briefly in boiling water and drain thoroughly. If using frozen spinach, drain well. Set aside.

2 Heat the oil in a karahi, wok or heavy pan and fry the onions with the curry leaves and the onion seeds for 1–2 minutes. Add the garlic, ginger, chilli powder, salt and ground coriander. Stir-fry for a further 2–3 minutes.

3 Add half the red pepper slices and all the mushrooms and continue to stir-fry for 2–3 minutes.

4 Add the spinach and stir-fry for 4–6 minutes, then add the fromage frais or ricotta and half the fresh coriander, followed by the remaining red pepper slices. Stir-fry for a further 2–3 minutes before serving, garnished with the remaining coriander.

Cook's Tip
Whether you use fresh or frozen spinach, make sure it is well drained, otherwise the stir-fried mixture will be too wet when you add the fromage frais or ricotta. Tip the spinach into a colander, and press it against the sides of the colander with a wooden spoon to extract as much liquid as possible.

Spiced Coconut Mushrooms

Here is a simple and delicious way to cook mushrooms. They can be served with almost any Indian meal, as well as with traditional Western grilled or roasted vegetables.

Serves 4

30ml/2 tbsp groundnut
  (peanut) oil
2 garlic cloves, finely chopped
2 fresh red chillies, seeded
  and sliced into rings
3 shallots, finely chopped
225g/8oz/3 cups brown cap
  (cremini) mushrooms,
  thickly sliced
150ml/¼ pint/⅔ cup
  coconut milk
30ml/2 tbsp chopped fresh
  coriander (cilantro)
salt and ground black pepper

1 Heat a karahi, wok or shallow pan until hot, add the oil and swirl it around. Add the garlic and chillies, then stir-fry for a few seconds.

2 Add the shallots and stir-fry them for 2–3 minutes until softened. Add the mushrooms and stir-fry for 3 minutes.

3 Pour in the coconut milk and bring to the boil. Boil rapidly over a high heat until the liquid has reduced by about half and coats the mushrooms. Season to taste with salt and pepper.

4 Sprinkle over the chopped coriander and toss the mushrooms gently to mix. Serve immediately.

Variations
• *Use chopped fresh chives instead of chopped fresh coriander (cilantro), if you wish.*
• *White (button) mushrooms or field (portabello) mushrooms would also work well instead of brown cap (cremini) mushrooms.*
• *Sprinkle some chopped toasted cashew nuts over the mushrooms before serving, if you like.*

Energy 67kcal/280kJ; Fat 5.9g; Saturated fat 1.2g; Carbohydrate 2.4g; Fibre 0.8g.

Energy 188kcal/778kJ; Fat 11.57g; Saturated fat 5.99g; Carbohydrate 14.71g; Fibre 4.68g.

Courgettes with Mushrooms in a Yogurt Sauce

The slightly tart flavour of natural yogurt makes a wonderfully creamy sauce which is delicious with cooked mushrooms and courgettes.

Serves 4
15ml/1 tbsp oil
1 medium onion, roughly chopped
5ml/1 tsp ground coriander
5ml/1 tsp ground cumin
5ml/1 tsp salt
2.5ml/½ tsp chilli powder

225g/8oz/3 cups mushrooms, sliced
2 courgettes (zucchini), sliced
45ml/3 tbsp natural (plain) low-fat yogurt
15ml/1 tbsp chopped fresh coriander (cilantro)

1 Heat the oil in a heavy pan and fry the onion until golden brown. Lower the heat to medium, add the ground coriander, cumin, salt and chilli powder and stir together well.

2 Once the onion and the spices are well blended, add the mushrooms and courgettes, and stir-fry gently for about 5 minutes until soft. If the mixture is too dry, add just a little water to loosen.

3 Finally, add the yogurt and mix it well into the vegetables.

4 Sprinkle with chopped fresh coriander and serve immediately.

Cook's Tip
Yogurt has a great affinity with stir-fried vegetables, and this lovely combination of sliced mushrooms and courgettes (zucchini) would make a tasty accompaniment to serve with aubergine (eggplant) dishes.

Stuffed Okra

A delicious accompaniment to any dish, this can also be served on a bed of strained yogurt which gives an excellent contrast in flavour.

Serves 4–6
225g/8oz large okra
15ml/1 tbsp mango powder (amchur)

2.5ml/½ tsp ground ginger
2.5ml/½ tsp ground cumin
2.5ml/½ tsp chilli powder (optional)
2.5ml/½ tsp turmeric
a few drops of vegetable oil
30ml/2 tbsp cornflour (cornstarch), placed in a plastic bag
vegetable oil, for frying
salt

1 Wash the okra and dry on kitchen paper. Carefully trim off the tops without making a hole. Using a sharp knife, make a slit lengthways in the centre of each okra but do not cut all the way through.

2 In a bowl, mix the mango powder, ginger, cumin, chilli if using, turmeric and salt with a few drops of oil. Leave the mixture to rest for 1–2 hours.

3 Using your fingers, part the slit of each okra carefully and fill each with as much of the spice filling as possible.

4 Put all the okra into the plastic bag with the cornflour and shake the bag carefully to coat the okra evenly.

5 Fill a frying pan with enough oil to sit 2.5cm/1in deep, heat it and fry the okra in small batches for about 5–8 minutes, or until they are brown and slightly crisp. Serve hot.

Cook's Tip / Variation
Dusting the okra in cornflour before frying helps to ensure that none of the sticky liquid escapes and keeps the pods perfectly crisp.

Energy 64kcal/265kJ; Fat 3.70g; Saturated fat 0.58g; Carbohydrate 4.80g; Fibre 1.40g.

Energy 176kcal/734kJ; Fat 12.4g; Saturated fat 1.6g; Carbohydrate 15.5g; Fibre 2.3g.

Okra in Yogurt

This tangy vegetable dish can be served as an accompaniment, but it could also make an excellent vegetarian meal if served with tarka dhal and warm, freshly made chapatis.

Serves 4

450g/1lb okra
15ml/1 tbsp oil
2.5ml/½ tsp onion seeds
3 medium fresh green chillies, chopped
1 medium onion, sliced
1.5ml/¼ tsp ground turmeric
2.5ml/½ tsp salt
15ml/1 tbsp natural (plain) low-fat yogurt
2 medium tomatoes, sliced
15ml/1 tbsp chopped fresh coriander (cilantro)
chapatis, to serve

1 Wash and trim the okra, cut into 1cm/½in pieces and place in a bowl. Set aside.

2 Heat the oil in a medium, heavy pan, add the onion seeds, green chillies and onion, and fry for about 5 minutes until the onion has turned golden brown.

3 Reduce the heat. Add the ground turmeric and salt to the onions and fry for about 1 minute.

4 Next, add the prepared okra, turn the heat to medium-high and quickly stir-fry the okra until they are lightly golden.

5 Stir in the yogurt, tomatoes and, finally, the coriander. Cook for a further 2 minutes.

6 Transfer the okra to a serving dish and serve immediately with freshly made chapatis.

Cook's Tip
It is always wise to wear plastic or rubber gloves when preparing chillies as they contain a strong irritant that will sting open cuts or eyes if it comes into contact with them.

Energy 82kcal/342kJ; Fat 4.2g; Saturated fat 0.41g; Carbohydrate 7.6g; Fibre 5.3g.

Masala Okra

Okra, or "lady's fingers", are a very popular Indian vegetable. Here the pods are stir-fried with a dry masala mixture to make a tasty side dish.

Serves 4

450g/1lb okra
2.5ml/½ tsp ground turmeric
5ml/1 tsp chilli powder
15ml/1 tbsp ground cumin
15ml/1 tbsp ground coriander
1.5ml/¼ tsp salt
1.5ml/¼ tsp granulated sugar
15ml/1 tbsp lemon juice
30ml/2 tbsp chopped fresh coriander (cilantro)
15ml/1 tbsp oil
2.5ml/½ tsp cumin seeds
2.5ml/½ tsp black mustard seeds
chopped fresh tomatoes, to garnish
poppadums, to serve

1 Wash, dry and trim the stalks away from the top of the okra, being careful not to pierce the pod itself, otherwise the sticky juices will be released and will affect the final dish. Set the okra aside. In a bowl, mix together the turmeric, chilli powder, cumin, ground coriander, salt, sugar, lemon juice and fresh coriander.

2 Heat the oil in a large, heavy pan. Add the cumin seeds and mustard seeds, and fry for about 2 minutes or until they start to splutter.

3 Scrape in the spice mixture and continue to fry for 2 minutes.

4 Add the okra, cover and cook over a low heat for 10 minutes, or until tender. Garnish with chopped fresh tomatoes and serve with poppadums.

Cook's Tip
When buying okra, choose firm, brightly coloured pods that are less than 10cm/4in long; larger ones can be stringy.

Energy 102kcal/424kJ; Fat 5.4g; Saturated fat 0.4g; Carbohydrate 8.6g; Fibre 4.7g.

Stir-fried Paneer with Mushrooms & Peas

Indian cheese, known as paneer, is a very versatile ingredient. It is used in both sweet and savoury dishes. Indian housewives generally make this cheese at home, although in recent years it has become available commercially.

Serves 4–6
90ml/6 tbsp ghee or vegetable oil
225g/8oz paneer, cubed
1 onion, finely chopped
a few fresh mint leaves, chopped, plus extra sprigs to garnish
50g/2oz/1 cup chopped fresh coriander (cilantro)
3 fresh green chillies, chopped
3 garlic cloves
2.5cm/1in piece fresh root ginger, sliced
5ml/1 tsp ground turmeric
5ml/1 tsp chilli powder (optional)
5ml/1 tsp garam masala
225g/8oz/3 cups tiny button (white) mushrooms, washed
225g/8oz/2 cups frozen peas, thawed
175ml/6fl oz/¾ cup natural (plain) yogurt, mixed with 5ml/1 tsp cornflour (cornstarch)
salt

1 Heat the ghee or oil in a karahi, wok or large pan, and fry the paneer cubes until they are golden brown on all sides. Remove and drain on kitchen paper.

2 Grind the onion, mint, coriander, chillies, garlic and ginger with a mortar and pestle or in a food processor to a fairly smooth paste. Remove and mix in the turmeric, chilli powder, if using, and garam masala, with salt to taste.

3 Remove the excess ghee or oil from the pan, leaving about 15ml/1 tbsp. Heat and fry the paste over a medium heat for 8–10 minutes, or until the raw onion smell disappears and the oil separates. Add the mushrooms, peas and paneer and mix well. Cool the mixture slightly and fold in the yogurt. Simmer for about 10 minutes, until the vegetables are tender and the flavours are well mixed. Garnish with fresh mint and serve.

Corn on the Cob in a Rich Onion Sauce

Corn is grown extensively in the Punjab region, where it is used in many delicacies. Corn bread, *makki ki roti*, along with spiced mustard greens, *sarson ka saag*, is a combination that is hard to beat and it is what the Punjabis thrive on. Here, corn is cooked in a thick, rich onion sauce, in another classic Punjabi dish. It is excellent served with naan bread.

Serves 4–6
4 corn on the cob, thawed if frozen
vegetable oil, for frying
1 large onion, finely chopped
2 garlic cloves, crushed
5cm/2in piece fresh root ginger, crushed
2.5ml/½ tsp ground turmeric
2.5ml/½ tsp onion seeds
2.5ml/½ tsp cumin seeds
2.5ml/½ tsp chilli powder
6–8 curry leaves
2.5ml/½ tsp granulated sugar
200ml/7fl oz/scant 1 cup natural (plain) yogurt
chilli powder, to taste

1 Cut each corn cob in half, using a heavy knife or cleaver to make clean cuts and avoid damaging the kernels.

2 Heat the oil in a karahi, wok or large pan and fry the corn until golden brown. Remove the corn and set aside. Remove any excess oil, leaving about 30ml/2 tbsp in the wok.

3 Grind the onion, garlic and ginger to a paste using a mortar and pestle or in a food processor. Transfer the paste to a bowl and mix in the spices, curry leaves and granulated sugar.

4 Heat the oil and fry the onion paste mixture over a low heat for 8–10 minutes until all the spices have blended well and the oil separates from the sauce.

5 Cool the onion paste mixture and fold in the yogurt. Mix to a smooth sauce. Add the corn and mix well, so that all the pieces are covered with the sauce. Reheat gently for about 10 minutes. Serve hot.

Energy 280kcal/1162kJ; Fat 19.9g; Saturated fat 3.7g; Carbohydrate 11.7g; Fibre 3.7g.

Energy 214kcal/888kJ; Fat 15.1g; Saturated fat 2g; Carbohydrate 15.9g; Fibre 1.5g.

Sweet Cinnamon Carrots

A honey and cinnamon coating makes these glazed carrots extra special.

Serves 4

450g/1lb carrots, peeled and cut into batons
25g/1oz/2 tbsp butter
2.5ml/½ tsp ground cinnamon
15ml/1 tbsp clear honey
15ml/1 tbsp chopped fresh coriander (cilantro)
salt and ground black pepper
sprig of fresh coriander, to garnish

1 Steam or boil the carrots for 5 minutes until crisply tender. Drain well and return to the pan.

2 Add the butter to the pan to melt and add the cinnamon and honey. Season to taste with salt and pepper.

3 Add the chopped fresh coriander and toss well to coat the carrots with the flavoured butter. Serve garnished with a sprig of fresh coriander.

Sweet-&-sour Onions

Cooked in this way, sweet baby onions make an unusual yet tasty side dish.

Serves 6

450g/1lb baby onions, peeled
50ml/2fl oz/¼ cup wine vinegar
45ml/3 tbsp olive oil
40g/1½oz/⅓ cup caster (superfine) sugar
45ml/3 tbsp tomato purée (paste)
1 bay leaf
2 parsley sprigs
65g/2½oz/½ cup raisins
salt and ground black pepper

1 Put all the ingredients in a pan with 300ml/½ pint/1¼ cups water. Bring to the boil and simmer gently, uncovered, for 45 minutes or until the onions are tender and most of the liquid has evaporated.

2 Remove the bay leaf and parsley, check the seasoning and transfer to a serving dish. Serve at room temperature.

Spicy Bitter Gourds

Bitter gourds are widely used in India, often combined with other vegetables in a curry. They are also known as karelas and resemble small cucumbers with a warty skin. Gourds that are about 10cm/4in long are usually slightly less bitter than the tiny ones.

Serves 4

675g/1½lb bitter gourds
15ml/1 tbsp oil
2.5ml/½ tsp cumin seeds
6 spring onions (scallions), finely chopped
5 tomatoes, finely chopped
2.5cm/1in piece fresh root ginger, finely chopped
2 garlic cloves, crushed
2 fresh green chillies, finely chopped
2.5ml/½ tsp chilli powder
5ml/1 tsp ground coriander
5ml/1 tsp ground cumin
45ml/3 tbsp soft dark brown sugar
15ml/1 tbsp gram flour
fresh coriander (cilantro) sprigs, to garnish
salt

1 Bring a large pan of lightly salted water to the boil. Peel the bitter gourds and halve them. Discard the seeds. Cut into 2cm/¾in pieces, then cook in the boiling water for about 10–15 minutes or until just tender. Drain well.

2 Heat the oil in a large, heavy pan and fry the cumin seeds for 2 minutes until they begin to splutter.

3 Add the spring onions and fry for 3–4 minutes. Add the tomatoes, ginger, garlic and chillies, and cook the mixture, stirring occasionally, for a further 5 minutes.

4 Add 2.5ml/½ tsp salt, the remaining spices and sugar to the pan and cook for a further 2–3 minutes. Add the bitter gourds to the pan and mix well.

5 Sprinkle over the gram flour. Cover and simmer over a low heat for 5–8 minutes or until all the gram flour has been absorbed into the sauce. Stir well, then serve garnished with fresh coriander sprigs.

Top: Energy 97kcal/402kJ; Fat 5.5g; Saturated fat 3.4g; Carbohydrate 11.8g; Fibre 2.7g.
Above: Energy 150kcal/628kJ; Fat 5.8g; Saturated fat 0.8g; Carbohydrate 24.1g; Fibre 2g.

Energy 120kcal/490kJ; Fat 3.5g; Saturated fat 0.41g; Carbohydrate 9.2g; Fibre 0.4g.

Green Beans with Corn

Frozen green beans are useful for this dish, as they are quick to cook. It makes an excellent vegetable accompaniment.

Serves 4

15ml/1 tbsp oil
1.5ml/¼ tsp mustard seeds
1 medium red onion, diced
50g/2oz/⅓ cup frozen corn
50g/2oz/¼ cup canned red
   kidney beans, drained
175g/6oz frozen green beans
1 fresh red chilli, seeded
   and diced
1 garlic clove, chopped
2.5cm/1in piece fresh root ginger,
   finely chopped
15ml/1 tbsp chopped fresh
   coriander (cilantro)
5ml/1 tsp salt
1 medium tomato, seeded and
   diced, to garnish

1 Heat the oil in a karahi, wok or heavy pan for about 30 seconds, then add the mustard seeds and onion. Stir-fry for 2–3 minutes.

2 Add the corn, red kidney beans and green beans. Stir-fry for 3–5 minutes.

3 Add the red chilli, chopped garlic and ginger, coriander and salt, and stir-fry for 2–3 minutes.

4 Remove the pan from the heat. Transfer the vegetables to a serving dish and garnish with the diced tomato.

Cook's Tip
This is a good stand-by dish as it uses frozen and canned ingredients. To make sure you have always got a chilli available for making this dish, or others like it, you can freeze whole fresh chillies, washed but not blanched.

Vegetables & Beans with Curry Leaves

Bright, shiny green curry leaves look like small bay leaves, although they are not as tough. A popular seasoning ingredient in Indian cooking, curry leaves add a spicy flavour to dishes such as this dry vegetable and bean curry.

Serves 4

3 fresh green chillies
1 medium carrot
50g/2oz green beans
1 medium red (bell) pepper
15ml/1 tbsp oil
6 curry leaves
3 garlic cloves, sliced
3 dried red chillies
1.5ml/¼ tsp onion seeds
1.5ml/¼ tsp fenugreek
   seeds
115g/4oz/½ cup drained
   canned red kidney beans
5ml/1 tsp salt
30ml/2 tbsp lemon juice

1 Cut the chillies in half lengthways. Remove the membranes and seeds and chop the flesh.

2 Cut the carrot into strips and slice the green beans diagonally. Remove the seeds and stalk from the pepper and cut the flesh into strips.

3 Heat the oil in a karahi, wok or deep heavy pan. Add the curry leaves, sliced garlic cloves, dried chillies, and onion and fenugreek seeds.

4 When these ingredients turn a shade darker, add the chillies, kidney beans, carrot strips, green beans and pepper strips, stirring constantly.

5 Stir in the salt and the lemon juice. Lower the heat, cover and cook for about 5 minutes.

6 Transfer the hot curry to a serving dish and serve immediately.

Energy 84kcal/349kJ; Fat 3.44g; Saturated fat 0.5g; Carbohydrate 11.13g; Fibre 2.7g.

Energy 79kcal/331kJ; Fat 3.3g; Saturated fat 0.37g; Carbohydrate 9.7g; Fibre 2.6g.

Kidney Bean Curry

This is a popular Punjabi-style dish using red kidney beans. You can replace the dried beans with a 400g/14oz can if you prefer. Other pulses also work well in this dish.

Serves 4

225g/8oz/scant 1 cup dried red kidney beans
30ml/2 tbsp oil
2.5ml/½ tsp cumin seeds
1 onion, thinly sliced
1 fresh green chilli, finely chopped
2 garlic cloves, crushed
2.5cm/1in piece fresh root ginger, grated
30ml/2 tbsp curry paste
5ml/1 tsp ground cumin
5ml/1 tsp ground coriander
2.5ml/½ tsp chilli powder
2.5ml/½ tsp salt
400g/14oz can chopped tomatoes
30ml/2 tbsp chopped fresh coriander (cilantro)

1 Leave the kidney beans to soak overnight in a bowl of cold water.

2 Drain the beans and put in a large pan with double the volume of water. Boil vigorously for 10 minutes. Skim off any scum. Cover and cook for 1–1½ hours or until the beans are soft. If you want to reduce the cooking time, cook the beans in a pressure cooker for 20–25 minutes. Alternatively, replace the dried beans with canned beans. Use a 400g/14oz can and drain it very thoroughly.

3 Meanwhile, heat the oil in a large, heavy frying pan and fry the cumin seeds for 2 minutes until they begin to splutter. Add the onion, chilli, garlic and ginger, and fry for 5 minutes. Stir in the curry paste, cumin, ground coriander, chilli powder and salt, and cook for 5 minutes.

4 Add the tomatoes and simmer for 5 minutes. Drain the beans and stir them in with the fresh coriander, reserving a little of the herb for the garnish. Cover and cook for 15 minutes, adding a little water if necessary. Serve garnished with the reserved fresh coriander.

Mung Beans with Potatoes

Small mung beans are one of the quicker-cooking pulses. They do not require soaking and are easy and convenient to use. In this recipe they are cooked with potatoes and Indian spices to give a tasty and nutritious dish.

Serves 4

175g/6oz/1 cup mung beans
750ml/1¼ pints/3 cups water
225g/8oz potatoes, cut into 2cm/¾in chunks
30ml/2 tbsp oil
2.5ml/½ tsp cumin seeds
1 fresh green chilli, finely chopped
1 garlic clove, crushed
2.5cm/1in piece fresh root ginger, finely chopped
1.5ml/¼ tsp ground turmeric
2.5ml/½ tsp chilli powder
5ml/1 tsp salt
5ml/1 tsp granulated sugar
4 curry leaves
5 tomatoes, peeled and finely chopped
15ml/1 tbsp tomato purée (paste)
curry leaves, to garnish
plain rice, to serve

1 Wash the beans. Pour the water into a pan, add the beans and bring to the boil. Boil hard for 15 minutes, then reduce the heat, cover the pan and simmer until soft, about 30 minutes cooking time. Drain.

2 In a separate pan, par-boil the potatoes in boiling water for 10 minutes, then drain well.

3 Heat the oil in a heavy pan and fry the cumin seeds until they splutter. Add the chilli, garlic and ginger, and fry for 3–4 minutes.

4 Add the turmeric, chilli powder, salt and sugar, and cook for 2 minutes, stirring to prevent the mixture from sticking to the pan.

5 Add the 4 curry leaves, chopped tomatoes and tomato purée, and simmer for about 5 minutes until the sauce thickens. Mix the tomato sauce and the potatoes with the mung beans and heat through. Garnish with the extra curry leaves and serve with plain boiled rice.

Energy 258kcal/1087kJ; Fat 7.8g; Saturated fat 0.86g; Carbohydrate 33.7g; Fibre 11.7g.

Energy 254kcal/1070kJ; Fat 6.8g; Saturated fat 0.89g; Carbohydrate 36.9g; Fibre 6.3g.

Yogurt Salad

If this salad looks and tastes familiar, it isn't surprising. It is very similar to coleslaw, except that yogurt is used instead of mayonnaise, and cashew nuts are added.

Serves 4
115g/4oz cabbage
350ml/12fl oz/1½ cups natural (plain) low-fat yogurt
10ml/2 tsp clear honey
2 medium carrots, thickly sliced

2 spring onions (scallions), roughly chopped
50g/2oz/⅓ cup sultanas (golden raisins)
50g/2oz/½ cup cashew nuts (optional)
16 white grapes, halved
2.5ml/½ tsp salt
5ml/1 tsp chopped fresh mint

1 Use a mandolin, if you have one, to shred the cabbage finely. Alternatively, use a sharp knife to slice through the layers of the cabbage.

2 Using a fork, beat the yogurt in a bowl with the honey.

3 In a separate bowl, which will be suitable for serving the salad, mix together the carrots, spring onions, cabbage, sultanas, cashew nuts (if you are using them), grapes, salt and the chopped fresh mint.

4 Pour the sweetened yogurt mixture over the salad, mix well and serve.

Variation
For Squash and Yogurt Salad, mix together 2.5ml/½ tsp dry mustard, 2.5ml/½ tsp ground cumin, 2.5ml/½ tsp salt, 5ml/ 1 tsp grated fresh root ginger and 150ml/¼ pint/⅔ cup natural yogurt. Chop half a green (bell) pepper and add to the spicy yogurt. Peel 250g/9oz butternut squash, then slice it and boil or steam until tender. Add to the yogurt mixture and stir well.

Energy 119kcal/503kJ; Fat 0.9g; Saturated fat 0.49g; Carbohydrate 23.4g; Fibre 1.8g.

Nutty Salad

The smooth creamy dressing is perfect with the crunchy nuts.

Serves 4
150g/5oz can red kidney beans
1 medium onion, cut into 12 rings
1 medium green courgette (zucchini), sliced
1 medium yellow courgette (zucchini), sliced
50g/2oz/⅔ cup pasta shells, cooked
50g/2oz/½ cup cashew nuts

25g/1oz/¼ cup peanuts
fresh coriander (cilantro) and lime wedges, to garnish

For the dressing
115g/4oz/½ cup low-fat fromage frais or ricotta cheese
30ml/2 tbsp natural (plain) low-fat yogurt
1 fresh green chilli, chopped
15ml/1 tbsp chopped fresh coriander (cilantro)
salt and ground black pepper
2.5ml/½ tsp crushed dried red chillies
15ml/1 tbsp lemon juice

1 Drain the kidney beans. Arrange them with the onion rings, courgette slices and pasta in a salad dish and sprinkle the cashew nuts and peanuts over the top.

2 In a separate bowl, mix together the fromage frais or ricotta cheese, yogurt, green chilli, fresh coriander and salt and pepper to taste. Beat well using a fork until all the ingredients are thoroughly combined. You may find it easier to add the coriander leaves a few at a time and mix in, to allow their flavour to permeate the mixture and ensure the resulting dressing is smooth in texture.

3 Sprinkle the crushed red chillies and lemon juice over the dressing. Garnish the salad with fresh coriander and lime wedges, and serve with the dressing.

Cook's Tip
Make the dressing just before serving the salad, so that the flavour of the coriander will be at its most intense.

Energy 199kcal/829kJ; Fat 11.6g; Saturated fat 2.63g; Carbohydrate 15.2g; Fibre 2.9g.

Spinach & Mushroom Salad

This salad is especially good served with garlic-based vegetable dishes.

fresh coriander (cilantro) sprigs and lime slices, to garnish (optional)

Serves 4
10 baby corn cobs
115g/4oz/3 cups mushrooms
2 medium tomatoes
20 small spinach leaves
8–10 onion rings
salt and ground black pepper

1 Halve the baby corn cobs and slice the mushrooms and tomatoes.

2 Arrange all the salad ingredients in a large serving bowl. Season with salt and pepper and garnish with fresh coriander and lime slices, if you like.

Tofu & Cucumber Salad

This is a nutritious and refreshing salad with a hot, sweet-and-sour dressing. It is ideal for a buffet.

Serves 4–6
1 small cucumber
oil, for frying
1 square fresh or 115g/4oz long-life tofu
115g/4oz beansprouts, trimmed and rinsed
salt

For the dressing
1 small onion, grated
2 garlic cloves, crushed
2.5ml/½ tsp chilli powder
30–45ml/2–3 tbsp dark soy sauce
15–30ml/1–2 tbsp rice wine vinegar
10ml/2 tsp dark brown sugar
salt
celery leaves, to garnish

1 Trim the ends from the cucumber and then cut it into neat cubes.

2 Sprinkle the trimmed cucumber with salt and set aside while you prepare the remaining ingredients.

3 Heat a little oil in a pan and fry the tofu on both sides until golden brown. Drain well on absorbent kitchen paper and cut into cubes.

4 Prepare the dressing by blending together the onion, garlic and chilli powder. Stir in the soy sauce, vinegar, sugar and salt to taste. You can do this in a screw-topped glass jar.

5 Just before serving, rinse the cucumber under cold running water. Drain and dry thoroughly.

6 Toss the cucumber, tofu and beansprouts together in a serving bowl and pour over the dressing. Garnish with the celery leaves and serve immediately.

Baby Vegetable Salad with a Chilli Dressing

Warm salads make a pleasant change, and the flavours of the dressing are enhanced. Take the opportunity in spring to use the new season's baby vegetables for this mouthwatering combination, which makes an excellent accompaniment to spicy vegetarian meals.

Serves 6
10 baby potatoes, halved
15 baby carrots

10 baby courgettes (zucchini)
115g/4oz/1½ cups button (white) mushrooms

For the dressing
45ml/3 tbsp lemon juice
25ml/1½ tbsp oil
15ml/1 tbsp chopped fresh coriander (cilantro)
5ml/1 tsp salt
2 fresh green chillies, finely sliced

1 Boil the potatoes, carrots and courgettes in water until tender. Drain them and place in a serving dish with the mushrooms.

2 Make the dressing in a separate bowl. Mix together the lemon juice, oil, fresh coriander, salt and chillies.

3 Toss the vegetables thoroughly in the chilli dressing and transfer to a serving bowl.

Variation
For a mild version of this dish replace the green chillies with finely chopped green (bell) pepper.

Cook's Tip
As well as looking extremely attractive, the tiny baby vegetables give this salad a lovely flavour. Other baby vegetables, such as leeks, baby corn or cauliflower florets, can be used just as well.

Energy 73kcal/308kJ; Fat 3.1g; Saturated fat 0.39g; Carbohydrate 10.1g; Fibre 1.5g.

Top: Energy 25kcal/103kJ; Fat 0.6g; Saturated fat 0.09g; Carbohydrate 2.8g; Fibre 1.8g.
Above: Energy 65kcal/269kJ; Fat 4.6g; Saturated fat 0.6g; Carbohydrate 3.7g; Fibre 0.5g.

Mango, Tomato & Red Onion Salad

This salad makes a delicious appetizer. The under-ripe mango blends well with the tomato.

Serves 4
1 firm under-ripe mango
2 large tomatoes or 1 beefsteak
  tomato, sliced
1/2 red onion, sliced into
  rings
1/2 cucumber, peeled and thinly
  sliced
chopped chives, to garnish

For the dressing
30ml/2 tbsp vegetable oil
15ml/1 tbsp lemon juice
1 garlic clove, crushed
2.5ml/1/2 tsp hot pepper sauce
salt and ground black pepper

1 Using a sharp knife or peeler, remove the skin from the mango, then cut and slice the flesh into bite-size pieces.

2 Arrange the mango, tomatoes, onion and cucumber on a large serving plate.

3 Make the dressing. Blend the oil, lemon juice, garlic, pepper sauce and seasoning in a blender or food processor, or shake vigorously in a small screw-top jar.

4 Spoon the dressing over the salad. Garnish with the chopped chives and serve.

Cook's Tip
When cutting a mango, first peel the skin off with a sharp knife or peeler. Next, cut the fleshy cheeks from each side. Trim carefully around the fruit, following the curvature of the stone (pit), to remove all the flesh. You will end up with the stone, two cheeks and two thinner strips of fruit, which can then be sliced.

Peppery Bean Salad

This pretty salad uses canned beans for speed and convenience.

Serves 4–6
425g/15oz can red kidney beans
425g/15oz can black-eyed beans
  (peas)
425g/15oz can chickpeas
1/4 red (bell) pepper
1/4 green (bell) pepper
6 radishes
15ml/1 tbsp chopped spring onion
  (scallion), plus extra to garnish

For the dressing
5ml/1 tsp ground cumin
15ml/1 tbsp tomato ketchup
30ml/2 tbsp olive oil
15ml/1 tbsp white wine
  vinegar
1 garlic clove, crushed
2.5ml/1/2 tsp hot pepper
  sauce

1 Drain the red kidney beans, black-eyed beans and chickpeas, and rinse under cold running water. Shake off the excess water and tip them into a large bowl.

2 Core, seed and chop the red and green peppers. Trim the radishes and slice thinly. Add the peppers, radishes and spring onion to the bowl.

3 To make the dressing, mix together the cumin, tomato ketchup, oil, white wine vinegar and crushed garlic in a small bowl. Add a little salt and hot pepper sauce to taste, and stir again thoroughly to combine.

4 Pour the dressing over the salad and mix. Cover the salad and chill for at least 1 hour before serving, garnished with the sliced spring onion.

Cook's Tip
Look out for cans of mixed beans at the supermarket. These contain a colourful medley and would be perfect for this salad.

Energy 89kcal/370kJ; Fat 5.8g; Saturated fat 0.7g; Carbohydrate 8.6g; Fibre 1.9g.

Energy 430kcal/1814kJ; Fat 9.3g; Saturated fat 1.3g; Carbohydrate 64.8g; Fibre 19.8g.

Sweet Potato & Carrot Salad

This warm salad has a piquant flavour. If made as a main course, it will serve two.

Serves 4
1 medium sweet potato
2 carrots, cut into thick
  diagonal slices
3 medium tomatoes
8–10 iceberg lettuce leaves
75g/3oz/1/2 cup drained canned
  chickpeas

For the dressing
15ml/1 tbsp clear honey
90ml/6 tbsp natural (plain)
  low-fat yogurt
2.5ml/1/2 tsp salt
5ml/1 tsp coarsely ground
  black pepper

For the garnish
15ml/1 tbsp walnuts
15ml/1 tbsp sultanas
  (golden raisins)
1 small onion, cut into rings

1 Peel and dice the sweet potato. Cook in boiling water until soft but not mushy, remove from the heat, cover the pan and set aside.

2 Cook the carrots in a pan of boiling water for just a few minutes, making sure that they remain crunchy. Add the carrots to the sweet potatoes.

3 Drain the water from the sweet potatoes and carrots and mix them together in a bowl.

4 Slice the tops off the tomatoes, then scoop out and discard the seeds. Roughly chop the flesh.

5 Line a glass bowl with the lettuce leaves. Add the carrots, chickpeas and tomatoes to the potatoes and carrots. Mix lightly, then spoon the mixture into the lettuce-lined bowl.

6 Put all the dressing ingredients in a screw-top jar and shake well to combine, or put in a bowl and beat using a fork.

7 Garnish the salad with the walnuts, sultanas and onion rings. Pour the dressing over the salad or serve it in a separate bowl.

Energy 127kcal/532kJ; Fat 3.7g; Saturated fat 0.47g; Carbohydrate 20.6g; Fibre 3.1g.

Spicy Potato Salad

This tasty salad is quick to prepare, and makes a satisfying accompaniment to any selection of grilled or barbecued vegetables.

Serves 6
900g/2lb potatoes
2 red (bell) peppers
2 celery sticks
1 shallot
2 or 3 spring onions (scallions)
1 fresh green chilli
1 garlic clove, crushed

10ml/2 tsp finely chopped
  fresh chives
10ml/2 tsp finely chopped
  fresh basil
15ml/1 tbsp finely chopped
  fresh parsley
30ml/2 tbsp single (light) cream
45ml/3 tbsp mayonnaise
5ml/1 tsp prepared mild mustard
7.5ml/1 1/2 tsp granulated sugar
salt
chopped fresh chives, to garnish

1 Peel the potatoes. Boil in salted water for 10–12 minutes, until tender. Drain and cool, then cut into cubes and place in a large mixing bowl.

2 Halve the peppers, cut away and discard the core and seeds and cut the flesh into small pieces. Finely chop the celery, shallot and spring onions and slice the chilli very thinly, discarding the seeds. Add the vegetables to the potatoes together with the garlic and herbs.

3 Mix the cream, mayonnaise, mustard and sugar in a small bowl, stirring until the mixture is well combined.

4 Pour the dressing over the salad and stir gently to coat evenly. Serve, garnished with the chopped chives.

Cook's Tip
New potatoes would also work deliciously well in this recipe. Scrub them lightly to remove any earth and, unless they are very small, halve them. Cook them until just tender; test them with a knife.

Energy 185kcal/777kJ; Fat 6.7g; Saturated fat 1.3g; Carbohydrate 29.3g; Fibre 2.6g.

Spiced Yogurt

Yogurt is always a welcome accompaniment to hot curries. Here, it is topped with a hot spice mixture to provide a contrast in both taste and temperature.

Makes 450ml/¾ pint/ scant 2 cups
450ml/¾ pint/scant 2 cups
 natural (plain) yogurt
2.5ml/½ tsp freshly ground
 fennel seeds
salt
2.5ml/½ tsp granulated sugar
60ml/4 tbsp vegetable oil
1 dried red chilli
1.5ml/¼ tsp mustard seeds
1.5ml/¼ tsp cumin seeds
4–6 curry leaves
a pinch each of asafoetida and
 ground turmeric

1 In a heatproof serving dish, mix together the yogurt, fennel seeds, salt and sugar. Cover and chill until you are nearly ready to serve.

2 Heat the oil in a frying pan and fry the dried chilli, mustard and cumin seeds, curry leaves, asafoetida and turmeric.

3 When the chilli turns dark, pour the oil and spices over the yogurt. Fold the yogurt together with the spices at the table just before serving.

> **Variation**
> Asafoetida is quite bitter. Leave it out if you prefer.

> **Cook's Tip**
> You must keep asafoetida in an airtight container because its sulphurous odour will affect other foods and spices. It is most commonly available as a powder or granules, and is also sold in lumps that need to be crushed before using. It is a very powerful spice and should therefore be used in minute quantities. Even in its ground state, asafoetida lasts well over a year if stored properly, away from light and air.

Energy 36kcal/149kJ; Fat 2.6g; Saturated fat 0.4g; Carbohydrate 1.8g; Fibre 0g.

Grape & Walnut Raita

Refreshing raitas are served to cool the effect of hot curries. Cucumber and mint raita is the best known combination. Here is a refreshing fruit and nut version, which is particularly good with vegetable curries.

2 firm bananas
5ml/1 tsp granulated sugar
salt
5ml/1 tsp freshly ground
 cumin seeds
1.5ml/¼ tsp freshly roasted
 cumin seeds, chilli powder
 or paprika, to garnish

Serves 4
350ml/12fl oz/1½ cups
 natural (plain) yogurt
75g/3oz seedless grapes
50g/2oz/½ cup shelled
 walnuts

1 Place the yogurt in a chilled bowl and add the grapes and walnuts.

2 Slice the bananas directly into the bowl and fold in gently before they turn brown.

3 Add the sugar, salt and ground cumin, and gently mix together.

4 Chill, and just before serving, sprinkle on the cumin seeds, chilli powder or paprika.

> **Variations**
> • Instead of grapes, try kiwi fruit, peaches or nectarines.
> • Almonds or hazelnuts can be used instead of or as well as the walnuts.
> • For Coconut and Raisin Raita, coarsely grate half a fresh coconut by hand or using a food processor. Mix in a bowl with 225g/8oz natural (plain) yogurt and 2.5ml/½ tsp sugar. Stir in 25g/1oz chopped fresh coriander (cilantro) or mint, and add salt to taste. Transfer to a serving bowl.

Energy 184kcal/771kJ; Fat 9.6g; Saturated fat 1.2g; Carbohydrate 19.2g; Fibre 1g.

Sweet-&-sour Raita

This raita teams honey with mint sauce, chilli and fresh coriander to make a soothing mixture with underlying warmth. It goes well with biryanis.

Serves 4
475ml/16fl oz/2 cups natural (plain) low-fat yogurt
5ml/1 tsp salt
5ml/1 tsp granulated sugar
30ml/2 tbsp clear honey
7.5ml/1½ tsp mint sauce
30ml/2 tbsp roughly chopped fresh coriander (cilantro)
1 fresh green chilli, seeded and finely chopped
1 medium onion, diced
50ml/2fl oz/¼ cup water

1 Pour the yogurt into a bowl and whisk it well. Add the salt, sugar, honey and mint sauce.

2 Taste to check the sweetness and add more honey, if desired.

3 Reserve a little chopped coriander for the garnish and add the rest to the yogurt mixture, with the chilli, onion and water.

4 Whisk once again and pour into a serving bowl. Garnish with the reserved coriander and place in the refrigerator until ready to serve.

Variation
For Spinach Raita, finely chop 225g/8oz cooked spinach. Add to 450ml/¾ pint/scant 2 cups natural (plain) yogurt and mix in 2 chopped green chillies, 1.5ml/¼ tsp sugar, and salt and pepper to taste.

Cook's Tip
A 5–10cm/2–4in piece of peeled, seeded and grated cucumber can also be added to raita. Drain the cucumber in a colander, pressing it against the sides to extract excess liquid, which would dilute the raita.

Energy 128kcal/541kJ; Fat 1.18g; Saturated fat 0.64g; Carbohydrate 24.40g; Fibre 0.53g.

Sweet-&-sour Tomato & Onion Relish

This delicious relish can be served with any savoury meal. Choose vine-ripened tomatoes, if you can, as they have a superior flavour.

Serves 4
2 medium firm tomatoes
1 medium onion
1 fresh green chilli
15ml/1 tbsp fresh mint leaves
15ml/1 tbsp fresh coriander (cilantro) leaves
2.5ml/½ tsp Tabasco sauce
15ml/1 tbsp clear honey
2.5ml/½ tsp salt
30ml/2 tbsp lime juice
15ml/1 tbsp natural (plain) low-fat yogurt

1 Place the tomatoes in hot water for a few seconds. Lift each tomato out in turn, using a slotted spoon. The skins should have split, making it easy to remove them. Peel off carefully.

2 Cut the tomatoes in half, and squeeze out the seeds. Chop the flesh roughly. Set them aside while you prepare the other ingredients.

3 Using a sharp knife, roughly chop the onion, green chilli, mint and fresh coriander.

4 Place the herb mixture in a food processor with the Tabasco sauce, honey, salt and lime juice. Add the tomatoes to this and grind everything together for a few seconds.

5 Pour into a small serving bowl. Stir in the yogurt just before you serve the relish.

Cook's Tip
This relish will keep for up to 1 week in the refrigerator: prepare up to the end of step 4 but do not add the yogurt until just before you want to serve it.

Energy 43kcal/180kJ; Fat 0.29g; Saturated fat 0.06g; Carbohydrate 9.43g; Fibre 0.96g.

Fresh Coriander Relish

Delicious as an accompaniment to kebabs, samosas and bhajias, this relish can also be used as a spread for cucumber or tomato sandwiches.

Makes about 450g/1lb/ 2 cups

30ml/2 tbsp vegetable oil
1 dried red chilli
1.5ml/¼ tsp each cumin, fennel
   and onion seeds
1.5ml/¼ tsp asafoetida
4 curry leaves
115g/4oz/1⅓ cups desiccated
   (dry unsweetened shredded)
   coconut
10ml/2 tsp granulated sugar
salt
3 fresh green chillies, chopped
175–225g/6–8oz fresh coriander
   (cilantro), chopped
60ml/4 tbsp mint sauce
juice of 3 lemons

1 Heat the oil in a frying pan and add the dried chilli, the cumin, fennel and onion seeds, the asafoetida, curry leaves, desiccated coconut, sugar and salt. Fry, stirring often, until the coconut turns golden brown. Tip into a bowl and leave to cool.

2 Grind the spice mixture with the green chillies, fresh coriander and mint sauce. Moisten with lemon juice. Scrape into a bowl and chill before serving.

Cook's Tip
This may seem like a lot of coriander, but it is compacted when ground with the spices.

Variation
For Coriander and Walnut Relish, put 90ml/6 tbsp fresh coriander leaves, 2 garlic cloves, 50g/2oz chopped onion and 60ml/4 tbsp sugar into a food processor and grind until thick. Add 50g/2oz/½ cup chopped walnuts and mix well. Add salt and ground black pepper to taste.

Tomato Relish

This is a simple relish that can be served with most meals. It provides a contrast to hot curries, with its crunchy texture and refreshing ingredients.

Serves 4–6

2 small fresh green chillies
2 limes
2.5ml/½ tsp granulated sugar,
   or to taste
2 onions, finely chopped
4 firm tomatoes, finely chopped
½ cucumber, finely chopped
a few fresh coriander (cilantro)
   leaves, chopped
salt and ground black pepper
a few fresh mint leaves,
   to garnish

1 Using a sharp knife, cut both chillies in half. Scrape out the seeds, then chop the chillies finely and place them in a small bowl.

2 Squeeze the limes. Pour the juice into a glass bowl and add the sugar, with salt and pepper to taste. Set the bowl aside until the sugar and salt have dissolved, stirring the mixture occasionally.

3 Add the chopped chillies to the bowl, with the chopped onions, tomatoes, cucumber, chilli and fresh coriander leaves. Mix well.

4 Cover the bowl with clear film (plastic wrap) and place in the refrigerator for at least 3 hours, so that the flavours blend. Just before serving, taste the relish and add more salt, pepper or sugar if needed. Garnish with mint and serve.

Cook's Tip
For a milder flavour, use just one chilli, or dispense with the chilli altogether and substitute with a green (bell) pepper.

Energy 51kcal/211kJ; Fat 5.2g; Saturated fat 3.5g; Carbohydrate 0.8g; Fibre 0.9g.

Energy 47kcal/198kJ; Fat 0.5g; Saturated fat 0.1g; Carbohydrate 9.4g; Fibre 2.3g.

Fried Sesame Seed Chutney

This versatile chutney doubles as a dip, and also a sandwich filling with thin slices of cucumber.

Serves 4
175g/6oz/¾ cup sesame seeds
5ml/1 tsp salt
120–150ml/4–5fl oz/½–⅔ cup
    water
2 fresh green chillies, seeded
    and diced
60ml/4 tbsp chopped fresh
    coriander (cilantro)
15ml/1 tbsp chopped fresh
    mint
15ml/1 tbsp tamarind paste
30ml/2 tbsp granulated sugar
5ml/1 tsp oil
1.5ml/¼ tsp onion seeds
4 curry leaves
onion rings, sliced chillies and
    fresh coriander leaves,
    to garnish

1 Dry-roast the sesame seeds by putting them into a pan without adding any oil. Cook over medium to high heat, tossing them occasionally so that they brown evenly all over. Watch them carefully as they will burn if left. Leave the seeds to cool and then grind them in a coffee grinder until they become a grainy powder.

2 Transfer the sesame powder to a bowl. Add the salt, water, diced chillies, coriander, mint, tamarind paste and sugar, and use a fork to mix everything together.

3 Taste and adjust the seasoning, if necessary; the mixture should have a sweet-and-sour flavour. Add a little more tamarind paste if it needs to be more sour, or sugar to sweeten, if required.

4 Heat the oil in a heavy pan and fry the onion seeds and curry leaves together.

5 Tip the sesame seed paste into the pan and stir-fry for about 45 seconds. Transfer the chutney to a serving dish and leave to cool completely.

6 Garnish with onion rings, sliced green and red chillies and fresh coriander leaves and serve with your chosen curry.

Apricot Chutney

Chutneys can add zest to most meals, and in India you will usually find a selection of different kinds served in tiny bowls for people to choose from. Dried apricots are readily available from supermarkets and health food shops.

**Makes about 450g/1lb/
2 cups**
450g/1lb/2 cups dried apricots,
    finely diced
5ml/1 tsp garam masala
275g/10oz/1¼ cups soft
    light brown sugar
450ml/¾ pint/scant 2 cups
    malt vinegar
5ml/1 tsp grated fresh root
    ginger
5ml/1 tsp salt
75g/3oz/½ cup sultanas
    (golden raisins)
450ml/¾ pint/scant 2 cups
    water

1 Put the dried apricots and garam masala into a medium pan and add the light brown sugar, malt vinegar, ginger, salt, sultanas and water. Mix thoroughly with a spoon.

2 Bring to the boil, then reduce the heat and simmer for 30–35 minutes, stirring occasionally.

3 When the chutney has thickened to a fairly stiff consistency, spoon it into 2–3 clean jam jars and leave to cool. This chutney should be stored in the refrigerator.

Variation
For Orchard Fruit Chutney, put 675g/1½lb peeled, cored and chopped cooking apples into a large pan with 115g/4oz/¼ cup each dried peaches and apricots and 50g/2oz/scant ½ cup raisins. Chop 5 garlic cloves and grate a 5cm/2in piece of fresh root ginger and add them to the pan. Add 350g/12oz soft light brown sugar, 400ml/14fl oz/1⅔ cups malt vinegar, 10ml/2 tsp salt and 5ml/1 tsp cayenne pepper. Bring the mixture to the boil and simmer for 30 minutes, stirring frequently.

Energy 347kcal/1438kJ; Fat 28.31g; Saturated fat 4.03g; Carbohydrate 25.31g; Fibre 3.63g.

Energy 118kcal/506kJ; Fat 0.2g; Saturated fat 0g; Carbohydrate 29.7g; Fibre 2g.

Fresh Tomato & Onion Chutney

Chutneys are served with most dishes in Indian cuisine. This one is lightly seasoned, and perfect to accompany a heavily spiced vegetarian meal.

Serves 4
8 tomatoes
1 medium onion, chopped
45ml/3 tbsp light muscovado (brown) sugar
5ml/1 tsp garam masala
5ml/1 tsp ground ginger
175ml/6fl oz/¾ cup malt vinegar
5ml/1 tsp salt
15ml/1 tbsp clear honey
natural (plain) yogurt, sliced green chilli and fresh mint leaves, to garnish

1 Wash the tomatoes and cut them into quarters.

2 Place them with the onion in a heavy pan, and add the sugar, garam masala, ginger, vinegar, salt and honey.

3 Half-cover the pan with a lid and cook over a low heat for about 20 minutes.

4 Mash the tomatoes with a fork to break them up, then continue to cook them on a slightly higher heat until the chutney thickens.

5 Spoon the chutney into a bowl and leave to cool, then cover and place in the refrigerator until needed.

6 Serve chilled, garnished with yogurt, sliced chilli and mint leaves.

Cook's Tips
• This chutney will keep for about 2 weeks in a covered container in the refrigerator. Add the garnish when ready to serve.
• Malt vinegar is generally used for chutneys that require a rich flavour as it has a fuller flavour than white wine vinegar.
• The sugar and vinegar give the chutney its flavour as well as its keeping qualities.

Energy 118kcal/503kJ; Fat 0.66g; Saturated fat 0.18g; Carbohydrate 43.9g; Fibre 2.34g.

Tomato Chutney with Cinnamon & Nigella

This delicious relish is especially suited to lentil dishes. If kept in a covered bowl in the refrigerator, it will keep for a week.

Makes 450–500g/1–1¼lb/ 2–2¼ cups
90ml/6 tbsp vegetable oil
5cm/2in piece cinnamon stick
4 cloves
5ml/1 tsp freshly roasted cumin seeds
5ml/1 tsp nigella seeds
4 bay leaves
5ml/1 tsp mustard seeds, crushed
4 garlic cloves
800g/1¾lb canned, chopped tomatoes
5cm/2in piece fresh root ginger, crushed
5ml/1 tsp chilli powder
5ml/1 tsp ground turmeric
60ml/4 tbsp brown sugar

1 Pour the oil into a frying pan, karahi or wok and place over a medium heat. When the oil is hot, fry the cinnamon, cloves, cumin and nigella seeds, bay leaves and mustard seeds for about 5 minutes.

2 Crush the garlic cloves and add them to the spice mixture. Fry until golden. Meanwhile, drain the tomatoes, reserving the juices.

3 Add the ginger, chilli powder, turmeric, sugar and the reserved tomato juices. Simmer until reduced, add the tomatoes and cook for 15–20 minutes. Cool and serve.

Cook's Tip
Nigella seeds, or kalonji, are frequently used in Indian cooking. They are small black oval-shaped seeds that have a delicate, slightly peppery flavour a little like oregano. They are most often seen sprinkled over naan breads. They have a strong flavour so should be used sparingly in cooking. They add depth to the flavour of this chutney but can be omitted if you are unable to find them.

Energy 53kcal/224kJ; Fat 3.8g; Saturated fat 0.5g; Carbohydrate 4.8g; Fibre 0.4g.

Mint & Coconut Chutney

Makes about 350ml/
12fl oz/1½ cups
50g/2oz fresh mint leaves
90ml/6 tbsp desiccated (dry
  unsweetened shredded)
  coconut
15ml/1 tbsp sesame seeds
1.5ml/¼ tsp salt
175ml/6fl oz/¾ cup natural
  (plain) yogurt

1 Finely chop the fresh mint leaves, using a sharp kitchen knife.

2 Put the mint with the desiccated coconut, sesame seeds, salt and yogurt into a food processor or blender and process until smooth. Transfer the chutney to a sterilized jar, cover and chill until needed.

Tomato & Fresh Chilli Chutney

Makes about 475ml/
16fl oz/2 cups
1 red (bell) pepper
4 tomatoes, chopped
2 fresh green chillies, chopped
1 garlic clove, crushed
1.5ml/¼ tsp salt
2.5ml/½ tsp granulated sugar
5ml/1 tsp chilli powder
45ml/3 tbsp tomato purée
  (paste)
15ml/1 tbsp chopped fresh
  coriander (cilantro)

1 Halve the red pepper and remove the core and seeds. Roughly chop the red pepper halves.

2 Process the pepper with the tomatoes, chillies, garlic, salt, sugar, chilli powder, tomato purée and coriander with 30ml/ 2 tbsp water in a food processor until smooth. Transfer to a sterilized jar, cover and chill until needed.

> **Cook's Tip**
> *This chutney can be stored in the refrigerator for up to 5 days.*

Mango Chutney

Chutneys are usually served as an accompaniment to curry but this one is particularly nice served in a cheese sandwich or as a dip with poppadums.

Makes 450g/1lb/2 cups
60ml/4 tbsp malt vinegar
2.5ml/½ tsp crushed dried
  chillies
6 cloves
6 peppercorns
5ml/1 tsp roasted cumin seeds
2.5ml/½ tsp onion seeds
salt
175g/6oz/scant 1 cup
  granulated sugar
450g/1lb green (unripe) mangoes
5cm/2in piece fresh root ginger,
  thinly sliced
2 garlic cloves, crushed
thin rind of 1 orange or lemon
  (optional)

1 Use a sharp knife to cut two thick slices from either side of the large flat stone (pit) of the mango. Make criss-cross cuts in the flesh on each slice and then turn inside out. The cubes of flesh will stand proud of the skin. Cut these off close to the skin. Cut the remaining flesh from around the stone.

2 Pour the vinegar into a pan, and add the chillies, cloves, peppercorns, cumin and onion seeds, salt and sugar. Place over a low heat and simmer to infuse (steep) the spices in the vinegar – about 15 minutes.

3 Add the mango, ginger, garlic and peel, if using. Simmer until the mango is mushy and most of the vinegar has evaporated. When cool, pour into sterilized bottles. Cover and leave for a few days before serving.

> **Cook's Tip**
> *Fresh root ginger freezes very well, which can be handy if you find it difficult to get fresh ginger locally. It can be sliced or grated straight from the freezer and will thaw on contact with hot food.*

Energy 52kcal/224kJ; Fat 0g; Saturated fat 0g; Carbohydrate 13.7g; Fibre 0.7g.

Top: Energy 753kcal/3117kJ; Fat 66.6g; Saturated fat 50.2g; Carbohydrate 21.7g; Fibre 13.5g.
Above: Energy 187kcal/794kJ; Fat 2.5g; Saturated fat 0.5g; Carbohydrate 33.2g; Fibre 7.5g.

Pickled Onions

The English love of pickled onions is famous, and at the time of the Raj the popular pickle was introduced into India. They should be stored in a cool, dark place for at least 6 weeks before being eaten.

Makes 3 or 4 450g/1lb jars
1kg/2¼lb pickling onions
115g/4oz/½ cup salt

750ml/1¼ pints/3 cups malt vinegar
15ml/1 tbsp granulated sugar
2 or 3 dried red chillies
5ml/1 tsp brown mustard seeds
15ml/1 tbsp coriander seeds
5ml/1 tsp allspice berries
5ml/1 tsp black peppercorns
5cm/2in piece fresh root ginger, sliced
2 or 3 blades of mace
2 or 3 fresh bay leaves

1 Trim off the root end of each onion, but leave the onion layers attached. Cut a thin slice off the top (neck) end of each onion. Place the onions in a bowl, then cover with boiling water. Leave to stand for about 4 minutes, then drain. Peel off the skin from each onion with a small, sharp knife.

2 Place the peeled onions in a bowl and cover with cold water, then drain the water off and pour it into a large pan. Add the salt and heat slightly to dissolve it, then cool before pouring the brine over the onions. Cover the bowl with a plate and weigh it down slightly so that all the onions are submerged in the brine. Leave the onions to stand in the salted water for 24 hours.

3 Pour the vinegar into a large pan. Wrap all the remaining ingredients, except the bay leaves, in a piece of muslin (cheesecloth) or sew them into a coffee filter paper. Add to the vinegar with the bay leaves. Bring to the boil, simmer for 5 minutes, then remove from the heat. Leave to infuse (steep) overnight.

4 Drain the onions, rinse and pat dry. Pack them into sterilized jars. Add some or all of the spice from the vinegar, but not the ginger slices. The pickle will get hotter if you add the chillies. Pour the vinegar over the onions to cover and add the bay leaves. Cover the jars with non-metallic lids.

Energy 120kcal/500kJ; Fat 0.7g; Saturated fat 0g; Carbohydrate 26.3g; Fibre 4.7g.

Fresh Coconut Chutney with Onion & Chilli

Serve a bowl of this tasty fresh chutney as an accompaniment for any Indian-style main course.

Serves 4–6
200g/7oz fresh coconut, grated
3 or 4 fresh green chillies, seeded and chopped
20g/¾oz fresh coriander (cilantro), chopped, plus 2 or 3 sprigs to garnish
30ml/2 tbsp chopped fresh mint

30–45ml/2–3 tbsp lime juice
about 2.5ml/½ tsp salt
about 2.5ml/½ tsp caster (superfine) sugar
15–30ml/1–2 tbsp coconut milk (optional)
30ml/2 tbsp groundnut (peanut) oil
5ml/1 tsp nigella seeds
1 small onion, very finely chopped

1 Place the coconut, chillies, coriander and mint in a food processor. Add 30ml/2 tbsp of the lime juice, then process until thoroughly chopped.

2 Scrape the mixture into a bowl and add more lime juice to taste. Add salt and sugar to taste. If the mixture is dry, stir in 15–30ml/1–2 tbsp coconut milk.

3 Heat the oil in a small pan and fry the nigella seeds until they begin to pop, then reduce the heat and add the onion. Fry, stirring frequently, for 4–5 minutes, until the onion is soft.

4 Stir the onion mixture into the coconut mixture and leave to cool. Garnish with coriander before serving.

> **Cook's Tip**
> Nigella seeds, sometimes called black onion seeds or black cumin, can be found in Asian grocery stores, usually sold under the name kalonji.

Energy 168kcal/693kJ; Fat 17.2g; Saturated fat 11.1g; Carbohydrate 2.4g; Fibre 2.8g.

Red Onion, Garlic & Lemon Relish

This powerful relish is flavoured with spices and punchy preserved lemons. It reached India by way of Spain, being introduced by Jewish refugees forced to leave that country in the 15th century.

Serves 6
45ml/3 tbsp olive oil
3 large red onions, sliced
2 heads of garlic, separated into
 cloves and peeled
10ml/2 tsp coriander seeds,
 crushed but not finely ground
10ml/2 tsp light muscovado sugar,
 plus a little extra
pinch of saffron threads
5cm/2in piece cinnamon stick
2 or 3 small whole dried red
 chillies (optional)
2 fresh bay leaves
30–45ml/2–3 tbsp sherry vinegar
juice of 1/2 small orange
30ml/2 tbsp chopped preserved
 lemon
salt and ground black pepper

1 Heat the oil in a heavy pan. Add the onions and stir, then cover and reduce the heat to the lowest setting. Cook for 10–15 minutes, stirring occasionally, until the onions are soft and pale gold in colour.

2 Add the whole peeled garlic cloves and the crushed coriander seeds. Cover and cook for 5–8 minutes until the garlic is soft.

3 Add a pinch of salt, lots of pepper and the sugar. Stir, then cook, uncovered, for 5 minutes. Soak the saffron in about 45ml/3 tbsp warm water for 5 minutes, then add it to the onions, with the soaking water. Add the cinnamon stick, dried chillies, if using, and bay leaves. Stir in 30ml/2 tbsp of the sherry vinegar and the orange juice.

4 Cook over a low heat, uncovered, until the onions are very soft and most of the liquid has evaporated. Stir in the preserved lemon and cook gently for a further 5 minutes. Taste and adjust the seasoning, adding more salt, sugar and/or vinegar to taste. Serve warm or at room temperature. The relish tastes best if it is left to stand for 24 hours.

Onion, Mango & Peanut Chaat

Chaats are spiced relishes of vegetables and nuts, delicious with many savoury Indian dishes.

Serves 4
90g/3 1/2oz/scant 1 cup
 unsalted peanuts
15ml/1 tbsp peanut oil
1 onion, chopped
1/2 cucumber, seeded and diced
1 mango, peeled, stoned (pitted)
 and diced
1 fresh green chilli, seeded
 and chopped
30ml/2 tbsp chopped fresh
 coriander (cilantro)
15ml/1 tbsp chopped fresh
 mint
15ml/1 tbsp lime juice
pinch of light muscovado
 (brown) sugar

For the chaat masala
10ml/2 tsp ground toasted
 cumin seeds
2.5ml/1/2 tsp cayenne pepper
5ml/1 tsp mango powder
 (amchur)
2.5ml/1/2 tsp garam masala
a pinch of ground asafoetida
salt and ground black pepper

1 To make the chaat masala, grind all the spices together, then season with 2.5ml/1/2 tsp each salt and pepper.

2 Fry the peanuts in the oil until lightly browned, then drain on kitchen paper until cool.

3 Mix the onion, cucumber, mango, chilli, fresh coriander and mint in a bowl. Sprinkle in 5ml/1 tsp of the chaat masala. Stir in the peanuts and then add lime juice and/or sugar to taste. Set the mixture aside for 20–30 minutes for the flavours to mature.

4 Spoon the mixture into a serving bowl, sprinkle another 5ml/1 tsp of the chaat masala over and serve.

Cook's Tip
Any remaining chaat masala will keep in a sealed jar for 4–6 weeks.

Energy 107kcal/442kJ; Fat 5.8g; Saturated fat 0.8g; Carbohydrate 12g; Fibre 2.2g.

Energy 187kcal/776kJ; Fat 13.3g; Saturated fat 2.5g; Carbohydrate 11.1g; Fibre 2.9g.

Naan

Probably the most popular bread enjoyed with an Indian curry is naan, which was introduced from Persia. In Persian, the word "naan" means bread. Traditionally, naan is not rolled, but patted and stretched until the teardrop shape is achieved. You can, of course, roll it out to a circle, then gently pull the lower end, which will give you the traditional shape.

Makes 3

225g/8oz/2 cups unbleached strong white bread flour
2.5ml/½ tsp salt
15g/½oz fresh yeast
60ml/4 tbsp lukewarm milk
15ml/1 tbsp vegetable oil
30ml/2 tbsp natural (plain) yogurt
1 egg
30–45ml/2–3 tbsp melted ghee or butter, for brushing

1 Sift the flour and salt together into a large bowl. In a smaller bowl, cream the yeast with the milk. Set aside for 15 minutes. Add the yeast and milk mixture, vegetable oil, yogurt and egg to the flour. Combine the mixture using your hands until it forms a soft dough. Add a little more of the lukewarm water if the dough is too dry.

2 Turn the dough out on to a lightly floured surface and knead for about 10 minutes, or until it feels smooth. Return the dough to the bowl, cover and leave in a warm place for about 1 hour, or until it has doubled in size. Preheat the oven to its highest setting – it should not be any lower than 230°C/450°F/Gas 8.

3 Turn out the dough back on to the floured surface and knead for a further 2 minutes. Divide into three equal pieces, shape into balls and roll out into teardrop shapes 25cm/10in long, 13cm/5in wide and 5mm–8mm/¼–⅓in thick.

4 Preheat the grill (broiler) to its highest setting. Meanwhile, place the naan on preheated baking sheets and bake for 3–4 minutes, or until puffed up. Remove from the oven and place under the hot grill for a few seconds until the tops brown slightly. Brush with ghee or butter and serve warm.

Garlic & Coriander Naan

Traditionally cooked in a very hot clay oven known as a tandoor, naan are especially good when eaten with dry vegetable dishes.

Makes 3

275g/10oz/2½ cups unbleached strong white bread flour
5ml/1 tsp salt

5ml/1 tsp dried yeast
60ml/4 tbsp natural (plain) yogurt
15ml/1 tbsp melted butter or ghee, plus 30–45ml/2–3 tbsp for brushing
1 garlic clove, finely chopped
5ml/1 tsp black onion seeds
15ml/1 tbsp fresh coriander (cilantro)
10ml/2 tsp clear honey

1 Sift the flour and salt together into a large bowl. In a smaller bowl, cream the yeast with the yogurt. Set aside for 15 minutes. Add the yeast mixture to the flour with the smaller quantity of melted butter or ghee, and add the chopped garlic, black onion seeds and chopped coriander, mixing to a soft dough.

2 Tip out the dough on to a lightly floured surface and knead for about 10 minutes until smooth and elastic. Place in a lightly oiled bowl, cover with lightly oiled clear film (plastic wrap) and leave to rise in a warm place for 45 minutes, or until the dough has doubled in bulk.

3 Preheat the oven to 230°C/450°F/Gas 8. Place three heavy baking sheets in the oven to heat. Turn the dough out on to a lightly floured surface and knock back (punch down). Divide into three equal pieces and shape each into a ball.

4 Cover two of the balls of dough with oiled clear film and roll out the third into a teardrop shape about 25cm/10in long, 13cm/5in wide and about 5mm–8mm/¼–⅓in thick. Preheat the grill (broiler) to its highest setting. Place the single naan on the hot baking sheets and bake for 3–4 minutes, or until puffy.

5 Remove the naan from the oven and place under the hot grill for a few seconds or until browned slightly. Wrap in a dish towel to keep warm while you roll out and cook the remaining naan. Brush with melted butter or ghee and serve warm.

Energy 197kcal/830kJ; Fat 8.2g; Saturated fat 5g; Carbohydrate 29.2g; Fibre 1.2g.

Energy 326kcal/1378kJ; Fat 6.8g; Saturated fat 1.3g; Carbohydrate 59.7g; Fibre 2.3g.

Spiced Naan

Another excellent recipe for naan bread, this time with fennel seeds, onion seeds and cumin seeds.

Makes 6

450g/1lb/4 cups strong white
   bread flour
5ml/1 tsp baking powder
2.5ml/½ tsp salt
1 sachet easy-blend (rapid-rise)
   dried yeast
5ml/1 tsp caster (superfine) sugar

5ml/1 tsp fennel seeds
10ml/2 tsp onion seeds
5ml/1 tsp cumin seeds
150ml/¼ pint/⅔ cup hand-hot
   milk
30ml/2 tbsp oil, plus extra
   for brushing
150ml/¼ pint/⅔ cup natural
   (plain) yogurt
1 egg, beaten

1 Sift the flour, baking powder and salt into a mixing bowl. Stir in the yeast, sugar, fennel seeds, onion seeds and cumin seeds. Make a well in the centre. Stir the hand-hot milk into the flour mixture, then add the oil, yogurt and beaten egg. Mix to form a ball of dough.

2 Tip the dough out on to a lightly floured surface and knead it for 10 minutes until smooth. Return to the clean, lightly oiled bowl and roll the dough to coat it with oil. Cover the bowl with clear film (plastic wrap) and set aside in a warm place until the dough has doubled in bulk.

3 Put a heavy baking sheet in the oven and preheat the oven to 240°C/475°F/Gas 9. Also preheat the grill (broiler). Knead the dough again lightly and divide it into six pieces. Keep five pieces covered while working with the sixth. Quickly roll the piece of dough out to a teardrop shape, brush lightly with oil and slap the naan on to the hot baking sheet. Repeat with the remaining dough.

4 Bake the naan in the oven for 3 minutes until puffed up, then place the baking sheets under the grill for about 30 seconds or until the naan are lightly browned. Serve hot or warm as an accompaniment to an Indian curry.

Energy 294kcal/1248kJ; Fat 2.6g; Saturated fat 0.8g; Carbohydrate 61.3g; Fibre 2.3g.

Chapatis

A chapati is an unleavened bread made from chapati flour, a ground wholemeal flour known as *atta*, which is finer than the Western equivalent. An equal quantity of standard wholemeal flour and plain flour will also produce satisfactory results, although chapati flour is available from Indian grocers. This is the everyday bread of the Indian home.

Makes 8–10

225g/8oz/2 cups chapati flour
   or wholemeal (whole-wheat)
   flour
2.5ml/½ tsp salt
175ml/6fl oz/¾ cup water

1 Sift the flour and salt into a mixing bowl. Make a well in the centre and gradually stir in the water, mixing well with your fingers.

2 Form a supple dough and knead for 7–10 minutes. Ideally, cover with clear film (plastic wrap) and leave to one side for 15–20 minutes to rest.

3 Divide the dough into 8–10 equal portions. Roll out each piece to a circle on a well-floured surface.

4 Place a tava (chapati griddle) or heavy frying pan over a high heat. When steam rises from it, lower the heat to medium and add the first chapati to the pan.

5 When the chapati begins to bubble, turn it over. Press down with a clean dish towel or a flat spoon and turn once again.

6 Remove the cooked chapati from the pan and keep warm in a piece of foil lined with kitchen paper while you cook the other chapatis.

7 Repeat the process until all the breads are cooked. Serve hot.

Energy 96kcal/408kJ; Fat 0.4g; Saturated fat 0.1g; Carbohydrate 21.9g; Fibre 0.9g.

Red Lentil Pancakes

This is a type of *dosa*, which is essentially a pancake from southern India, but used in a similar fashion to north Indian bread.

Makes 6
150g/5oz/¾ cup long grain rice
50g/2oz/¼ cup red lentils
250ml/8fl oz/1 cup warm water

5ml/1 tsp salt
2.5ml/½ tsp ground turmeric
2.5ml/½ tsp ground black pepper
30ml/2 tbsp chopped fresh coriander (cilantro)
oil, for frying and drizzling

1 Place the rice and lentils in a large bowl, cover with the warm water, cover and soak for at least 8 hours or overnight.

2 Drain off the water and reserve. Place the rice and lentils in a food processor and blend until smooth. Blend in the reserved water. Scrape into a bowl, cover with clear film (plastic wrap) and leave in a warm place to ferment for about 24 hours.

3 Stir in the salt, turmeric, pepper and coriander. Heat a heavy frying pan over a medium heat for a few minutes until hot. Smear with oil and add about 30–45ml/2–3 tbsp batter.

4 Using the rounded base of a soup spoon, gently spread the batter out, using a circular motion, to make a pancake that is about 15cm/6in in diameter.

5 Cook in the pan for 1½–2 minutes, or until set. Drizzle a little oil over the pancake and around the edges. Turn over and cook for about 1 minute, or until golden brown. Keep the cooked pancakes warm in a low oven or on a plate over simmering water while cooking the remaining pancakes. Serve warm.

Variation
Add 60ml/4 tbsp grated coconut to the batter just before cooking for a richer flavour.

Parathas

Making a paratha is similar to making flaky pastry. The difference lies in the handling of the dough; this can be handled freely, unlike that for a flaky pastry.

Makes 12–15
350g/12oz/3 cups chapati flour or an equal quantity of wholemeal (whole-wheat) flour and plain (all-purpose) flour, plus 50g/2oz/½ cup for dusting

50g/2oz/½ cup plain (all-purpose) flour
5ml/1 tsp salt
40g/1½oz/3 tbsp ghee or unsalted (sweet) butter
water, to mix

1 Sift the flours and salt into a bowl. Make a well in the centre and add 10ml/2 tsp melted ghee or butter. Fold it into the flour to make a crumbly texture.

2 Gradually add water to make a soft, pliable dough. Knead until smooth. Cover and leave to rest for 30 minutes.

3 Melt the remaining ghee or butter over a low heat. Divide the dough into 12–15 equal portions and keep covered. Take one portion at a time and roll out on a lightly floured surface to about 10cm/4in in diameter.

4 Brush the dough with a little of the melted ghee or sweet butter and sprinkle with flour.

5 With a sharp knife, make a straight cut from the centre to the edge of the dough, then lift a cut edge and roll the dough into a cone shape. Lift it and flatten it again into a ball. Roll the dough out again on a lightly floured surface until it is 18cm/7in wide.

6 Heat a griddle and cook one paratha at a time, placing a little of the remaining ghee along the edges. Cook on each side until golden brown. Serve hot.

Energy 190kcal/798kJ; Fat 8.5g; Saturated fat 1.1g; Carbohydrate 26.1g; Fibre 0.5g.

Energy 123kcal/521kJ; Fat 2.8g; Saturated fat 1.4g; Carbohydrate 21.9g; Fibre 2.8g.

Tandoori Rotis

Roti means bread and is the most common food eaten in central and northern India. *Tandoori roti* is traditionally baked in a tandoor, or clay oven, but it can also be made successfully in an electric or gas oven at the highest setting.

Makes 6

350g/12oz/3 cups chapati
flour or wholemeal
(whole-wheat) flour
5ml/1 tsp salt
250ml/8fl oz/1 cup water
30–45ml/2–3 tbsp melted ghee
or unsalted (sweet) butter

1 Sift the flour and salt into a large mixing bowl. Add the water and mix to a soft, pliable dough.

2 Knead on a lightly floured surface for 3–4 minutes until smooth. Place the dough in a lightly oiled bowl, cover with lightly oiled clear film (plastic wrap) and leave to rest for about 1 hour.

3 Tip out the dough on to a lightly floured surface. Divide the dough into six pieces and shape each into a ball. Press out into a larger round with the palm of your hand, cover with lightly oiled clear film and leave to rest for about 10 minutes.

4 Meanwhile, preheat the oven to 230°C/450°F/Gas 8. Place three baking sheets in the oven to heat. Roll the rotis into 15cm/6in rounds, place two on each baking sheet and bake for 8–10 minutes. Brush with melted ghee or butter and serve warm.

> **Cook's Tip**
> *Chapati flour, known as atta, is a fine wholemeal flour used in Indian breads.*

Missi Rotis

This is a speciality from the Punjab. Gram flour, also known as besan, is used instead of the usual chapati flour. In the Punjab, *missi rotis* are very popular with a glass of lassi, a refreshing yogurt drink.

Makes 4

115g/4oz/1 cup gram flour
115g/4oz/1 cup wholemeal
(whole-wheat) flour
1 fresh green chilli, seeded
and chopped
1/2 onion, finely chopped
15ml/1 tbsp chopped fresh
coriander (cilantro)
2.5ml/1/2 tsp ground
turmeric
2.5ml/1/2 tsp salt
15ml/1 tbsp vegetable oil
120–150ml/4–5fl oz/1/2–2/3 cup
lukewarm water
30–45ml/2–3 tbsp melted
unsalted (sweet) ghee or butter

1 Mix the two types of flour, the chilli, onion, coriander, turmeric and salt together in a large bowl. Stir in the oil.

2 Mix in sufficient water to make a pliable soft dough. Tip out the dough on to a lightly floured surface and knead until smooth.

3 Place the dough in a lightly oiled bowl, cover with lightly oiled clear film (plastic wrap) and leave to rest for 30 minutes.

4 Place the dough on to a lightly floured surface. Divide into four equal pieces and shape into balls in the palms of your hands. Roll out each ball into a thick round about 15–18cm/6–7in in diameter.

5 Heat a griddle or heavy frying pan over a medium heat for a few minutes until hot.

6 Brush both sides of one roti with a little melted ghee or butter. Add it to the griddle or frying pan and cook for about 2 minutes, turning after 1 minute. Brush the cooked roti lightly with melted ghee or butter again, slide it on to a plate and keep warm in a low oven while cooking the remaining rotis in the same way. Serve the rotis warm.

Energy 226kcal/958kJ; Fat 3.5g; Saturated fat 0.5g; Carbohydrate 45.9g; Fibre 2g.

Energy 181kcal/769kJ; Fat 1.3g; Saturated fat 0.2g; Carbohydrate 37.3g; Fibre 5.3g.

Bhaturas

These leavened and deep-fried breads are from the Punjab, where the local people enjoy them with a bowl of spicy chickpea curry. The combination has become a classic over the years and is known as *choley bhature*. Bhaturas must always be eaten hot, and cannot be reheated.

Makes 10

15g/½oz fresh yeast
5ml/1 tsp granulated sugar
120ml/4fl oz/½ cup lukewarm
  water
200g/7oz/1¾ cups strong white
  bread flour
50g/2oz/⅓ cup semolina
2.5ml/½ tsp salt
15g/½oz/1 tbsp ghee or butter
30ml/2 tbsp natural (plain) yogurt
oil, for frying

1 Mix the yeast with the sugar and water in a jug (pitcher).

2 Sift the flour into a large bowl and stir in the semolina and salt. Rub in the butter or ghee.

3 Add the yeast mixture and yogurt, and mix to a dough. Turn out on to a lightly floured surface and knead for 10 minutes, or until smooth and elastic.

4 Place the dough in an oiled bowl, cover with oiled clear film (plastic wrap) and leave to rise in a warm place for about 1 hour, or until doubled in bulk.

5 Turn the dough out on to a lightly floured surface and knock back (punch down). Divide into ten equal pieces and shape each into a ball. Flatten into discs with the palm of your hand. Roll out on a lightly floured surface into 13cm/5in rounds.

6 Pour oil to a depth of 1cm/½in into a deep frying pan. Heat, and slide one bhatura into the oil. Fry for about 1 minute, turning over after 30 seconds.

7 Drain the bhatura well on kitchen paper. Keep each bhatura warm in a low oven while frying the remaining bhaturas. Serve immediately, while hot.

Pooris

These delicious little deep-fried breads, shaped into discs, make it temptingly easy to overindulge. In most areas, they are made of wholemeal flour, but in the east and north-east of India, they are made from plain refined flour, and are known as *loochis*.

Makes 12

115g/4oz/1 cup unbleached
  plain (all-purpose) flour
115g/4oz/1 cup wholemeal
  (whole-wheat) flour
2.5ml/½ tsp salt
2.5ml/½ tsp chilli powder
30ml/2 tbsp vegetable oil
100–120ml/3½–4fl oz/7–8 tbsp
  water
oil, for frying

1 Sift the flours, salt and chilli powder, if using, into a large mixing bowl. Add the vegetable oil then add sufficient water to mix to a dough.

2 Tip the dough out on to a lightly floured surface and knead for 8–10 minutes until smooth.

3 Place in an oiled bowl and cover with oiled clear film (plastic wrap). Leave for 30 minutes.

4 Place the dough on the floured surface. Divide into 12 pieces. Keeping the rest of the dough covered, roll one piece into a 13cm/5in round. Repeat with the remaining dough. Stack the pooris, layered between clear film, to keep them moist.

5 Pour the oil for frying to a depth of 2.5cm/1in in a deep frying pan and heat it to 180°C/350°F. Using a metal spatula, lift one poori and slide it into the oil; it will sink but then return to the surface and begin to sizzle. Gently press the poori into the oil. It will puff up. Turn the poori over after a few seconds and allow it to cook for a further 20–30 seconds.

6 Remove the poori from the pan and pat dry with kitchen paper. Place the cooked poori on a large baking tray and keep warm in a low oven while you cook the remaining pooris. Serve warm.

Energy 144kcal/605kJ; Fat 6.6g; Saturated fat 1.4g; Carbohydrate 19.7g; Fibre 0.7g.

Energy 79kcal/333kJ; Fat 2.2g; Saturated fat 0.3g; Carbohydrate 13.6g; Fibre 1.2g.

Ensaimadas

These sweet bread rolls are a popular snack, and can be made with various different fillings.

Makes 10–12

30ml/2 tbsp caster (superfine) sugar, plus extra for sprinkling
150ml/¼ pint/⅔ cup warm water
15ml/1 tbsp active dried yeast
450g/1lb/4 cups strong white bread flour
5ml/1 tsp salt
115g/4oz/½ cup butter, softened, plus 30ml/2 tbsp melted butter for the filling
4 egg yolks
90–120ml/6–8 tbsp warm milk
115g/4oz/1 cup grated Cheddar cheese (or similar well-flavoured hard cheese)

1 Dissolve 5ml/1 tsp of the sugar in the warm water, then sprinkle in the dried yeast. Stir, then set aside for 10 minutes or until frothy. Sift the flour and salt into a large bowl.

2 Cream the softened butter with the remaining sugar in a large bowl. When it is fluffy, beat in the egg yolks and a little of the sifted flour. Gradually stir in the remaining flour with the yeast mixture and enough milk to form a soft but not sticky dough. Transfer to an oiled plastic bag. Close the bag loosely, leaving plenty of room for the dough to rise. Leave in a warm place for about 1 hour, until the dough doubles in bulk.

3 On a lightly floured surface, knock back (punch down) the dough, then roll it out into a large rectangle. Brush the surface with half the melted butter, sprinkle with the cheese, then roll up from a long side like a Swiss (jelly) roll. Knead the dough thoroughly, then divide into 10–12 pieces.

4 Roll each piece of dough into a thin rope, 38cm/15in long. On greased baking sheets, coil each rope into a loose spiral. Leave to rise for about 45 minutes or until doubled in size. Preheat the oven to 220°C/425°F/Gas 7. Bake the ensaimadas for 15–20 minutes, until golden. Remove from the oven, then brush with the remaining melted butter and sprinkle with caster sugar. Serve warm.

Sugar Bread Rolls

These delicious sweet rolls make an unusual end to an Indian meal.

Makes 10

350g/12oz/3 cups strong white bread flour
5ml/1 tsp salt
15ml/1 tbsp caster (superfine) sugar
5ml/1 tsp dried yeast
150ml/¼ pint/⅔ cup hand-hot water
3 egg yolks
50g/2oz/¼ cup unsalted (sweet) butter, softened, plus 25g/1oz/ 2 tbsp extra
75g/3oz Cheddar cheese or Monterey Jack, grated
50g/2oz/¼ cup granulated sugar

1 Sift the flour, salt and caster sugar into a food processor fitted with a dough blade or the bowl of an electric mixer fitted with a dough hook. Make a well in the centre. Dissolve the yeast in the hand-hot water and pour into the well. Add the egg yolks and leave for a few minutes until bubbles appear on the surface of the liquid.

2 Mix the ingredients for 30–45 seconds to form a firm dough. Add the softened butter and knead for 2–3 minutes in a food processor, or for 4–5 minutes with an electric mixer, until smooth. Transfer the dough out to a floured bowl, cover and leave in a warm place to rise until doubled in bulk.

3 Transfer the dough to a lightly floured surface and divide it into 10 pieces. Spread the grated cheese over the surface. Roll each of the dough pieces into a 13cm/5in length, incorporating the cheese as you do so. Coil into snail shapes and place on a lightly greased high-sided tray measuring 30 × 20cm/12 × 8in.

4 Cover the rolls with clear film (plastic wrap) and leave in a warm place for 45 minutes or until doubled in bulk.

5 Preheat the oven to 190°C/375°F/Gas 5 and then bake the rolls for 20–25 minutes. Melt the remaining butter, brush it over the rolls, sprinkle with the sugar and allow to cool. Separate the rolls before serving.

Energy 327kcal/1372kJ; Fat 16.2g; Saturated fat 9.3g; Carbohydrate 38.6g; Fibre 1.4g.

Energy 235kcal/986kJ; Fat 9.5g; Saturated fat 5.9g; Carbohydrate 33.7g; Fibre 1.1g.

Melon & Strawberry Salad

A beautiful and colourful fruit salad, this is suitable to serve as a refreshing appetizer or to round off a rich and spicy meal. Don't be tempted to chill the salad; it tastes best at room temperature.

Serves 4
1 Galia or Ogen melon
1 honeydew melon or other
  melon of your choice
  (see Cook's Tip)
½ watermelon
225g/8oz/2 cups
  strawberries
15ml/1 tbsp lemon juice
15ml/1 tbsp clear honey
15ml/1 tbsp chopped
  fresh mint

1 Prepare the melons by cutting them in half and discarding the seeds by scraping them out with a spoon.

2 Use a melon baller to scoop out the flesh into balls or a knife to cut it into cubes. Place these in a fruit bowl.

3 Rinse and take the stems off the strawberries, twisting them so that they remove the hull at the same time. If the hull remains inside, use a fine, sharp knife to cut it out. Cut the fruit in half and add them to the bowl.

4 Mix together the lemon juice and honey and add 15ml/1 tbsp water to make this easier to pour over the fruit. Mix into the fruit gently.

5 Sprinkle the chopped mint over the top of the fruit and serve.

Cook's Tip
Use whichever melons are available: replace Galia or Ogen with cantaloupe melon, or replace watermelon with charentais, for example. Try to choose three melons with a variation in colour for an attractive effect.

Pears in Spiced Wine

Familiar Indian spices, infused in a red wine syrup, give pears a lovely warm flavour. The colour is beautiful, too.

Serves 4
1 bottle full-bodied red wine
1 cinnamon stick
4 cloves
2.5ml/½ tsp freshly grated
  nutmeg

2.5ml/½ tsp ground
  ginger
8 peppercorns
175g/6oz/scant 1 cup
  caster (superfine) sugar
thinly pared rind of ½ orange
thinly pared rind of ½ lemon
8 firm ripe pears

1 Pour the wine into a heavy pan into which the pears will fit snugly when standing upright.

2 Stir the cinnamon stick, cloves, nutmeg, ginger, peppercorns, caster sugar and citrus rinds into the wine.

3 Peel the pears, leaving the stalks intact, and stand them in the pan. The wine should only just cover the pears.

4 Bring the liquid to the boil, lower the heat, cover and simmer very gently for 30 minutes, or until the pears are tender. Using a slotted spoon, transfer the pears to a bowl.

5 Boil the poaching liquid until it has reduced by half and is thick and syrupy.

6 Strain the syrup over and around the pears and serve the dessert hot or cold.

Cook's Tip
Serve the pears with a mascarpone cream, made by combining equal quantities of mascarpone cheese and double (heavy) cream, and adding a little vanilla extract for flavour. They also taste good with yogurt or ice cream.

Energy 191kcal/806kJ; Fat 0.3g; Saturated fat 0g; Carbohydrate 43.1g; Fibre 6.6g.

Energy 114kcal/482kJ; Fat 0.7g; Saturated fat 0g; Carbohydrate 26.5g; Fibre 1.6g.

Spiced Fruit Salad

Exotic fruits are becoming increasinly commonplace in supermarkets these days, and it is fun to experiment with the different varieties. Look out in particular for physalis, star fruit, papaya and passion fruit.

Serves 4–6

75g/3oz/6 tbsp granulated
  sugar
300ml/½ pint/1¼ cups water
30ml/2 tbsp syrup from a jar
  of preserved stem ginger
2 pieces star anise
2.5cm/1in cinnamon
  stick
1 clove
juice of ½ lemon
2 fresh mint sprigs
1 mango
2 bananas, sliced
8 fresh or drained canned
  lychees
225g/8oz/2 cups strawberries,
  hulled and halved
2 pieces preserved stem ginger,
  cut into sticks
1 medium pineapple

1 Put the sugar, water, ginger syrup, star anise, cinnamon, clove, lemon juice and mint into a pan. Bring to the boil, then simmer for 3 minutes. Strain into a bowl and set aside to cool.

2 Remove the top and bottom from the mango and cut off the outer skin. Stand the mango on one end and remove the flesh in two pieces either side of the flat stone (pit). Slice evenly.

3 Add the mango slices to the syrup with the bananas, lychees, strawberries and stem ginger. Mix in well, making sure the fruits are well coated in the sugary liquid.

4 Cut the pineapple in half by slicing down the centre, using a very sharp knife. Loosen the flesh with a smaller, serrated knife, and remove the flesh by cutting around the rim and scooping it out. The pineapple halves will resemble two boat shapes. Do not discard the pineapple flesh, but cut it into chunks and add to the fruity syrup.

5 Spoon some of the fruit salad into the pineapple halves and serve on a large dish. There will be sufficient fruit salad in the bowl to refill the pineapple halves at least once.

Citrus Fruit Salad

This is a very appetizing and refreshing salad, with a typically Indian combination of citrus fruits seasoned with salt and pepper. It will provide the perfect ending to a heavy meal.

Serves 6

2 navel oranges
1 honeydew melon
½ watermelon
1 fresh mango
115g/4oz seedless green and
  black grapes
225g/8oz canned mandarin
  segments, drained
225g/8oz canned grapefruit
  segments, drained
juice of 1 lemon
salt and ground black pepper
2.5ml/½ tsp sugar
1.5ml/¼ tsp freshly ground
  cumin seeds

1 Using a sharp knife, cut a thin slice of peel and pith from each end of an orange. Place cut side down on a plate and cut off the peel and pith in strips. Remove any remaining pith. Cut out each segment leaving the membrane behind. Squeeze the remaining juice from the membrane. Repeat with the other orange.

2 Cut the honeydew melon in half and scrape out the seeds using a spoon. Remove the seeds from the watermelon in the same way. Use a melon baller to scoop out the flesh into balls or a knife to cut it into cubes.

3 Using a sharp knife take two thick slices from either side of the large flat stone (pit) of the mango without peeling the fruit. Make slices into the flesh and then turn the skin inside out. The slices of flesh will stand proud of the skin and can be easily cut off.

4 Place all the fruit in a large serving bowl and add the lemon juice. Toss gently to prevent damaging the fruit.

5 Mix together the remaining ingredients and sprinkle over the fruit. Gently toss, chill thoroughly and serve.

Energy 167kcal/710kJ; Fat 0.8g; Saturated fat 0.2g; Carbohydrate 39.5g; Fibre 3.1g.

Energy 110kcal/468kJ; Fat 0.3g; Saturated fat 0.1g; Carbohydrate 27.1g; Fibre 2.4g.

Mango & Coconut Stir-fry

Choose a ripe mango for this recipe. If you buy one that is a little underripe, leave it in a warm place for a day or two before using.

Serves 4

1/4 coconut

1 large, ripe mango

*juice and finely grated rind
  of 2 limes*
15ml/1 tbsp sunflower oil
15g/1/2oz/1 tbsp butter
30ml/2 tbsp clear honey
*crème fraîche or ice cream,
  to serve*

1 Prepare the coconut if necessary. Drain the milk and remove the flesh. Peel with a vegetable peeler so that it forms flakes.

2 Peel the mango. Cut the stone (pit) out of the middle of the fruit. Cut each half of the mango into slices. Place the mango slices in a bowl and pour over the lime juice and rind. Set aside.

3 Meanwhile heat a karahi or wok, then add 10ml/2 tsp of the oil. When the oil is hot, add the butter. Once the butter has melted, stir in the coconut flakes and stir-fry for 1–2 minutes until the coconut is golden brown. Remove and drain on kitchen paper. Wipe out the pan. Strain the mango slices, reserving the juice.

4 Heat the pan again and add the remaining oil. When the oil is hot, add the mango and stir-fry for 1–2 minutes, then add the juice and leave to bubble and reduce for 1 minute.

5 Stir in the honey. When it has dissolved, spoon the mango and its juices into one large serving bowl or individual dishes. Sprinkle on the stir-fried coconut flakes and serve with crème fraîche or ice cream.

Variation
Nectarine or peach slices can be used instead of the mango.

Stewed Pumpkin in Coconut Cream

Fruit stewed in coconut milk makes a deliciously fresh and sweet dessert. Pumpkins, bananas and melons can all be prepared in this simple but tasty way.

Serves 4–6

*1kg/2 1/4lb kabocha
  pumpkin*
*750ml/1 1/4 pints/3 cups
  coconut milk*
*175g/6oz/scant 1 cup
  granulated sugar*
pinch of salt
*4–6 fresh mint sprigs,
  to decorate*

1 Cut the pumpkin in half using a large, sharp knife, then cut away and discard the skin. Scoop out the seed cluster by scraping it out with a spoon.

2 Reserve a few seeds and throw away the remainder. Using a sharp knife, cut the pumpkin flesh into pieces that are about 5cm/2in long and 2cm/3/4in thick.

3 Pour the coconut milk into a pan. Add the sugar and salt, and bring to the boil.

4 Add the pumpkin and simmer for about 10–15 minutes, or until it is tender.

5 Serve warm, in individual dishes. Decorate each serving with a mint sprig and toasted pumpkin seeds (see Cook's Tip).

Cook's Tip
To make the decoration, wash the reserved pumpkin seeds to remove any fibres, then pat them dry on kitchen paper. Roast them in a dry frying pan without any oil, or spread them out on a baking sheet and grill (broil) until golden brown, tossing them frequently to prevent them from burning. Watch them carefully as they will burn if left. These seeds can be prepared in advance and used cold to decorate the stewed pumpkin.

Energy 357kcal/1478kJ; Fat 32.7g; Saturated fat 24.1g; Carbohydrate 13.8g; Fibre 7g.

Energy 246kcal/1051kJ; Fat 1.1g; Saturated fat 0.6g; Carbohydrate 60.4g; Fibre 2.5g.

Mangoes with Sticky Rice

Sticky rice is just as good in desserts as in savoury dishes, and mangoes, with their delicate fragrance and velvety flesh, complement it especially well. You need to start preparing this dish the day before you intend to serve it.

Serves 4
175ml/6fl oz/ ³⁄₄ cup thick
   coconut milk
115g/4oz/ ²⁄₃ cup white
   glutinous rice
45ml/3 tbsp granulated sugar
pinch of salt
2 ripe mangoes
strips of pared lime rind, to decorate

1 Pour the coconut milk into a bowl and leave to stand until the cream rises to the top.

2 Rinse the glutinous rice thoroughly in several changes of cold water until it runs clear, then leave to soak overnight in a bowl of fresh cold water.

3 Drain the rice well and spread it out evenly in a steamer lined with muslin (cheesecloth). Cover and steam over a double boiler or a pan of simmering water for about 20 minutes, or until the rice is tender.

4 Reserve 45ml/3 tbsp of the cream from the top of the coconut milk. Pour the remainder into a pan and add the sugar and salt. Heat, stirring constantly, until the sugar has dissolved, then bring to the boil. Remove the pan from the heat, pour the coconut milk into a bowl and leave to cool.

5 Tip the cooked rice into a bowl and pour over the cooled coconut milk mixture. Stir well, then leave the rice mixture to stand for 10–15 minutes.

6 Meanwhile, peel the mangoes, cut the flesh away from the central stones (pits) and cut into slices.

7 Spoon the rice on to individual serving plates. Arrange the mango slices on one side, then drizzle with the reserved coconut cream. Decorate with strips of lime rind and serve.

Energy 200kcal/846kJ; Fat 0.8g; Saturated fat 0.2g; Carbohydrate 46g; Fibre 2g.

Papayas in Jasmine Flower Syrup

The fragrant flower syrup can be prepared in advance, using fresh jasmine flowers from a houseplant or the garden. It tastes fabulous with papayas, but it is also good with all sorts of desserts. Try it with ice cream or spooned over lychees or mangoes.

Serves 2
105ml/7 tbsp water
45ml/3 tbsp palm sugar or
   light muscovado (brown)
   sugar
20–30 jasmine flowers, plus
   a few extra to decorate
   (optional)
2 ripe papayas
juice of 1 lime

1 Place the water and sugar in a small pan. Heat gently, stirring occasionally, until the sugar has dissolved, then simmer, without stirring, over a low heat for 4 minutes.

2 Pour into a bowl, leave to cool slightly, then add the jasmine flowers. Leave to infuse (steep) for at least 20 minutes.

3 Peel the papayas and slice in half lengthways. Scoop out and discard the seeds. Place the papayas on serving plates and squeeze over the lime.

4 Strain the syrup into a clean bowl, discarding the flowers. Spoon the syrup over the papayas. If you like, decorate with a few fresh jasmine flowers.

Variation
Slices of mango would work well in this recipe in place of papayas.

Cook's Tip
Although scented white jasmine flowers are perfectly safe to eat, it is important to be sure that they have not been sprayed with pesticides or other harmful chemicals. Washing them may not remove all the residue.

Energy 233kcal/990kJ; Fat 0.4g; Saturated fat 0g; Carbohydrate 58.7g; Fibre 8.8g.

Toffee Apples

A wickedly sweet way to end a meal, this dessert of crisp pieces of apple with a crunchy coating evokes memories of childhood.

Serves 4
4 firm eating apples
115g/4oz/1 cup plain
   (all-purpose) flour
about 120ml/4fl oz/½ cup water
1 egg, beaten
vegetable oil, for deep-frying, plus
   30ml/2 tbsp for the toffee
115g/4oz/½ cup granulated
   sugar

1 Peel and core each apple and cut into eight pieces. Dust each piece of apple with a little of the flour.

2 Sift the remaining flour into a mixing bowl, then slowly add the cold water and stir well to make a smooth batter.

3 Add the beaten egg and blend well.

4 Heat the oil in a karahi, wok or deep-fryer to a temperature of 190°C/375°F, or until a cube of bread dropped in the oil browns in about 45 seconds. Dip the apple pieces in the batter and deep-fry for about 3 minutes or until golden. Remove and drain on kitchen paper. Drain off the oil from the pan.

5 Heat the remaining oil in the pan, add the sugar and stir constantly until the sugar has caramelized. Quickly add the apple pieces and blend well so that each piece of apple is thoroughly coated with the toffee.

6 Dip the apple pieces in cold water to harden before serving.

> **Variation**
> Try this recipe with bananas or pineapple pieces for a delicious change.

Energy 410kcal/1723kJ; Fat 18.5g; Saturated fat 2.5g; Carbohydrate 60g; Fibre 2g.

Sesame Fried Fruits

For this deep-fried dessert you can use any firm fruit that are in season. Bananas are fantastic, but the batter also works well with pineapple and apple. Serve them as soon as they are fried so that they retain their crispness.

Serves 4
115g/4oz/1 cup plain
   (all-purpose) flour
2.5ml/½ tsp bicarbonate of soda
   (baking soda)
30ml/2 tbsp sugar
1 egg
90ml/6 tbsp water
15ml/1 tbsp sesame seeds
   or 30ml/2 tbsp desiccated
   (dry unsweetened shredded)
   coconut
4 firm bananas
oil, for deep-frying
salt
30ml/2 tbsp clear honey,
   to serve
fresh mint sprigs and lychees,
   to decorate

1 Sift the flour, bicarbonate of soda and a pinch of salt into a bowl. Stir in the sugar.

2 Whisk in the egg and just enough water to make a thin batter. Then whisk in the sesame seeds or the desiccated coconut.

3 Peel the bananas. Carefully cut each one in half lengthways, then cut in half crossways. Don't do this until you are ready to cook them, because once peeled, bananas will quickly discolour.

4 Heat the oil in a karahi, wok or deep-fryer to a temperature of 190°C/375°F, or until a cube of bread dropped in the oil browns in about 45 seconds. Dip the bananas in the batter, then gently drop a few pieces at a time into the hot oil. Fry until golden brown.

5 Remove the bananas from the oil and drain on kitchen paper.

6 Serve immediately with clear honey, and decorate with mint sprigs and lychees.

Energy 384kcal/1607kJ; Fat 20.7g; Saturated fat 6.3g; Carbohydrate 46g; Fibre 3g.

Coconut Fried Bananas

These deliciously sweet treats are a favourite with children and adults alike.

Serves 4

115g/4oz/1 cup plain (all-purpose) flour
2.5ml/½ tsp bicarbonate of soda (baking soda)
pinch of salt
30ml/2 tbsp granulated sugar
1 egg, beaten
90ml/6 tbsp water
30ml/2 tbsp desiccated (dry unsweetened shredded) coconut or 15ml/1 tbsp sesame seeds
4 firm bananas
vegetable oil, for deep-frying
fresh mint sprigs, to decorate
30ml/2 tbsp clear honey, to serve (optional)

1 Sift the flour, bicarbonate of soda and salt into a large bowl. Stir in the granulated sugar and the egg, and whisk in just enough of the water to make quite a thin batter.

2 Whisk the coconut or sesame seeds into the batter so that they are evenly distributed.

3 Peel the bananas. Carefully cut each one in half lengthways, then in half crossways to make 16 pieces of about the same size. Don't do this until you are ready to cook them because, once peeled, bananas will quickly discolour.

4 Heat the oil in a karahi, wok or deep-fryer to a temperature of 190°C/375°F or until a cube of bread, dropped in the oil, browns in about 45 seconds. Dip the banana pieces in the batter, then gently drop a few into the oil.

5 Deep-fry until golden brown, then lift out and drain well on kitchen paper.

6 Cook the remaining banana pieces in the same way. Serve immediately with honey, if using, and decorated with sprigs of fresh mint.

Deep-fried Bananas

Fry these bananas at the last minute, so that the outer crust of batter is crisp in texture and the banana is soft and warm inside.

Serves 8

115g/4oz/1 cup self-raising (self-rising) flour
40g/1½oz/⅓ cup rice flour
2.5ml/½ tsp salt
200ml/7fl oz /scant 1 cup water
finely grated lime rind
8 small bananas
oil for deep-frying
caster (superfine) sugar and 1 lime, cut into wedges, to serve

1 Sift the self-raising flour, the rice flour and the salt together into a bowl. Add just enough of the water to make a smooth, coating batter. Mix well, then stir in the lime rind.

2 Heat the oil in a karahi, wok or deep-fryer to a temperature of 190°C/375°F, or until a cube of bread dropped in the oil browns in about 45 seconds.

3 Peel the bananas and dip them into the batter two or three times.

4 Deep-fry the battered bananas in the hot oil until crisp and golden.

5 Drain and serve hot, dredged with sugar. Offer the lime wedges to squeeze over the bananas.

Variation

For Banana Fritters using evaporated (unsweetened condensed) milk, sift 115g/4oz/1 cup plain (all-purpose) flour and a pinch of salt into a bowl. Make a well in the centre and add 1 beaten egg. Blend the egg and the flour together, and as the mixture becomes thick, stir in a 175g/6oz can evaporated milk to make a smooth batter. Heat oil for deep-frying to 190°C/375°F and split 4 bananas in half lengthways. Dip them in the batter and deep-fry until golden. Roll in caster (superfine) sugar and serve.

Energy 412kcal/1725kJ; Fat 20.7g; Saturated fat 2.8g; Carbohydrate 53.4g; Fibre 2.3g.

Energy 201kcal/840kJ; Fat 10g; Saturated fat 1.3g; Carbohydrate 27.1g; Fibre 1.2g.

Fried Pineapple

A very simple and quick dessert – fresh pineapple fried in butter, brown sugar and lime juice, and sprinkled with toasted coconut. The slightly sharp taste of the fruit makes this a very refreshing treat at the end of a rich Indian meal.

Serves 4
1 pineapple
40g/1½oz/3 tbsp butter
15ml/1 tbsp desiccated (dry unsweetened shredded) coconut
60ml/4 tbsp soft light brown sugar
60ml/4 tbsp fresh lime juice
lime slices, to decorate
thick and creamy natural (plain) yogurt, to serve

1 Using a sharp knife, cut the top off the pineapple and peel off the skin, taking care to remove the eyes.

2 Cut the pineapple in half and remove and discard the woody core. Cut the flesh lengthways into 1cm/½in wedges.

3 Heat the butter in a large, heavy frying pan or wok. When it has melted, add the pineapple wedges and cook over a medium heat for 1–2 minutes on each side, or until they have turned pale golden in colour.

4 Meanwhile, dry-fry the desiccated coconut in a small frying pan until lightly browned. Remove the pan from the heat and set aside.

5 Sprinkle the soft light brown sugar into the pan with the pineapple, add the lime juice and cook, stirring constantly, until the sugar has dissolved.

6 Divide the pineapple wedges among four bowls, sprinkle with the coconut, decorate with the lime slices and serve with the yogurt.

Energy 238kcal/1004kJ; Fat 11g; Saturated fat 7.2g; Carbohydrate 36.2g; Fibre 2.9g.

Honeyed Apples

These scrumptious treats are best prepared for a select number as they require the cook's complete attention. The honey coating crispens when the fritters are dipped in iced water.

Serves 4–5
4 crisp eating apples
juice of ½ lemon
25g/1oz/¼ cup cornflour (cornstarch)
sunflower oil, for deep-frying
toasted sesame seeds, for sprinkling

For the fritter batter
115g/4oz/1 cup plain (all-purpose) flour
generous pinch of salt
120–150ml/4–5fl oz/½–⅔ cup water
30ml/2 tbsp sunflower oil
2 egg whites

For the sauce
250ml/8fl oz/1 cup clear honey
120ml/4fl oz/½ cup sunflower oil
5ml/1 tsp white wine vinegar

1 Peel, core and cut the apples into eighths, brush each piece lightly with lemon juice then dust with cornflour.

2 To make the sauce, heat the honey and oil in a pan, stirring continuously until blended. Remove from the heat and stir in the white wine vinegar.

3 Sift the flour and salt into a bowl, then stir in the water and oil. Whisk the egg whites until stiff peaks form and then fold them into the batter.

4 Heat the oil in a karahi, wok or deep-fryer to a temperature of 190°C/375°F, or until a cube of bread dropped in the oil browns in about 45 seconds. Spear each piece of apple in turn on a skewer, dip in the batter and fry in the hot oil until golden. Drain on kitchen paper. Place the fritters in a dish and pour the sauce over.

5 Transfer the fritters to a lightly oiled serving dish, and sprinkle with the toasted sesame seeds. Serve the honeyed fritters at once, offering bowls of iced water for dipping to crispen the honey coating.

Energy 564kcal/2361kJ; Fat 32.8g; Saturated fat 3.9g; Carbohydrate 67.8g; Fibre 2g.

Kheer

Both Muslim and Hindu communities prepare kheer, which is traditionally served in mosques and temples.

Serves 4–6

15g/½oz/1 tbsp ghee
5cm/2in piece cinnamon stick
175g/6oz/¾ cup soft brown sugar
115g/4oz/1 cup coarsely ground rice

1.2 litres/2 pints/5 cups full cream (whole) milk
5ml/1 tsp ground cardamom
50g/2oz/⅓ cup sultanas (golden raisins)
25g/1oz/¼ cup flaked (sliced) almonds
2.5ml/½ tsp freshly grated nutmeg, to serve

1 In a heavy pan, melt the ghee and fry the cinnamon stick and soft brown sugar. Watch carefully while frying and when the sugar begins to caramelize reduce the heat immediately, or remove the pan from the heat, as sugar can burn very quickly.

2 Return the pan to the heat and add the rice and half the milk. Bring to the boil, stirring constantly to avoid the milk boiling over. Reduce the heat and simmer until the rice is cooked, stirring regularly.

3 Stir in the remaining milk, with the ground cardamom, sultanas and almonds. Leave to simmer until the mixture thickens, stirring constantly to prevent the kheer from sticking to the base of the pan, about 1½ hours.

4 When the mixture is thick and creamy, spoon it into a serving dish or individual dishes. Serve the kheer hot or cold, sprinkled with the freshly grated nutmeg. Decorate with tinfoil, if you like.

Cook's Tip
Kheer is traditionally cooked twice: once until the rice grains disintegrate and then with the spices and flavourings. This recipe uses ground rice and so it will take less time to cook.

Sweet Fried Loops

These irresistible fritters are delicious served with hot chocolate or coffee.

Makes about 24

450ml/15fl oz/scant 2 cups water
15ml/1 tbsp olive oil

15ml/1 tbsp caster (superfine) sugar, plus extra for dredging
2.5ml/½ tsp salt
150g/5oz/1¼ cups plain (all-purpose) flour
1 large egg
sunflower oil, for deep-frying

1 Mix the water, oil, sugar and salt in a large pan and bring to the boil. Remove from the heat, and then sift in the flour. Beat well with a wooden spoon until smooth.

2 Beat in the egg to make a smooth, glossy mixture with a piping consistency. Spoon into a pastry bag fitted with a large star nozzle.

3 Heat the oil in a karahi, wok or deep-fryer to a temperature of 190°C/375°F, or until a cube of bread dropped in the oil browns in about 45 seconds. Pipe loops of the mixture, two at a time, into the hot oil. Cook the loops for 3–4 minutes until they are golden.

4 Lift out the loops with a wire skimmer or slotted spoon and drain them on kitchen paper. Dredge them with caster sugar and serve warm.

Variation
Add 2.5ml/½ tsp cinnamon to the caster (superfine) sugar for sprinkling, if you like, to give the loops a warm, spicy flavour.

Cook's Tip
If you don't have a piping bag, you could fry teaspoons of mixture in the same way. Don't try to fry too many fritters at a time as they swell a little during cooking.

Energy 588kcal/2463kJ; Fat 20.6g; Saturated fat 11.1g; Carbohydrate 90.6g; Fibre 0.7g.

Energy 122kcal/507kJ; Fat 10.9g; Saturated fat 1.4g; Carbohydrate 5.5g; Fibre 0.2g.

Ground Rice Pudding

This delicious and light ground rice pudding is the perfect end to a spicy Indian meal. It can be served either hot or cold.

Serves 4–6
50g/2oz/½ cup coarsely ground rice
4 green cardamom pods, crushed

900ml/1½ pints/3¾ cups semi-skimmed (low-fat) milk
90ml/6 tbsp granulated sugar
15ml/1 tbsp rose water
15ml/1 tbsp crushed pistachio nuts, to garnish

1 Place the ground rice in a pan with the cardamom pods.

2 Add 600ml/1 pint/2½ cups of the milk and bring to the boil over a medium heat, stirring occasionally.

3 Add the remaining milk and stir over a medium heat for about 10 minutes, or until the rice mixture thickens to a creamy consistency.

4 Stir in the sugar and rose water and continue to cook for a further 2 minutes.

5 Garnish with the pistachio nuts and serve.

Variation
For an even richer version of this pudding, you could add 40g/1½oz ground almonds to the rice at step 1.

Cook's Tip
Rose water is a distillation of scented rose petals which has the intense fragrance and flavour of roses. It is a popular flavouring in Indian cooking. Use it cautiously, adding just enough to suit your taste.

Black Rice Pudding

This unusual rice pudding, flavoured with fresh root ginger, is quite delicious. When cooked, black rice still retains its husk and has a nutty texture. Serve in small bowls, with a little coconut milk or cream poured over each helping.

1cm/½in piece fresh root ginger, bruised
50g/2oz/¼ cup soft dark brown sugar
50g/2oz/¼ cup granulated sugar
300ml/½ pint/1¼ cups coconut milk or cream, to serve

Serves 6
115g/4oz/generous ½ cup black glutinous rice
475ml/16fl oz/2 cups water

1 Put the black glutinous rice in a sieve (strainer) and rinse well under cold running water.

2 Drain and put in a large pan, with the water. Bring to the boil and stir to prevent the rice from settling on the base of the pan. Cover and cook for about 30 minutes.

3 Add the ginger and both the brown and white sugar.

4 Cook for a further 15 minutes, adding a little more water if necessary, until the rice is cooked and porridge-like.

5 Remove the ginger and serve warm, in bowls, topped with coconut milk or cream.

Cook's Tip
Although black glutinous rice looks similar to wild rice, which is the seed of a rush plant, it is in fact a true rice. It has a particularly nutty flavour that is ideal for puddings and cakes. Long cooking makes the pudding thick and creamy, as the rice is naturally sticky.

Energy 260kcal/1102kJ; Fat 5.8g; Saturated fat 2.53g; Carbohydrate 46g; Fibre 0.3g.

Energy 146kcal/616kJ; Fat 0.5g; Saturated fat 0.1g; Carbohydrate 34.2g; Fibre 0g.

Baked Rice Pudding

Black glutinous rice, also known as black sticky rice, has long dark grains and a nutty taste reminiscent of wild rice. This baked pudding has a distinct character and flavour all of its own, as well as an intriguing and enticing appearance.

Serves 4–6

175g/6oz/scant 1 cup white or black glutinous rice
30ml/2 tbsp soft light brown sugar
475ml/16fl oz/2 cups coconut milk
250ml/8fl oz/1 cup water
3 eggs
30ml/2 tbsp granulated sugar

1 Combine the glutinous rice and brown sugar in a pan. Pour in half the coconut milk and the water.

2 Bring to the boil, reduce the heat to low and simmer, stirring occasionally, for 15–20 minutes, or until the rice has absorbed most of the liquid. Preheat the oven to 150°C/300°F/Gas 2.

3 Spoon the rice mixture into a single, large ovenproof dish or divide it among individual ramekins. Beat the eggs with the remaining coconut milk and sugar in a bowl.

4 Strain the egg mixture into a jug (pitcher), then pour it evenly over the par-cooked rice in the dish or ramekins.

5 Place the dish or individual ramekins in a roasting pan. Carefully pour in enough hot water to come halfway up the sides of the dish or ramekins.

6 Cover with foil and bake for about 35–60 minutes, or until the custard has set. Serve warm or cold.

> **Cook's Tip**
> *Throughout South-east Asia, black glutinous rice is usually used for sweet dishes, whereas its white counterpart is more often used in savoury recipes.*

Traditional Indian Vermicelli

Indian vermicelli, made from wheat, is much finer than Italian vermicelli and has a good texture in desserts. It is available from Asian stores.

Serves 4

115g/4oz/1 cup Indian vermicelli
1.2 litres/2 pints/5 cups water
2.5ml/½ tsp saffron threads
15ml/1 tbsp granulated sugar
60ml/4 tbsp low-fat fromage frais or Greek (US strained plain) yogurt, to serve

15ml/1 tbsp flaked (sliced) almonds
15ml/1 tbsp chopped pistachio nuts
15ml/1 tbsp granulated sugar

To decorate
15ml/1 tbsp shredded fresh or desiccated (dry unsweetened shredded) coconut

1 Crush the vermicelli in your hands and place it in a pan. Pour in the water, add the saffron and bring to the boil. Boil for about 5 minutes.

2 Stir in the sugar and continue cooking until the water has evaporated. Press through a sieve (strainer), if necessary, to remove any excess liquid.

3 Place the vermicelli in a serving dish and decorate with the coconut, almonds, pistachio nuts and sugar. Serve with fromage frais or yogurt.

> **Cook's Tip**
> *You can use a variety of fruits instead of nuts to garnish this dessert. Try a few soft fruits such as blackberries, raspberries or strawberries, or add some chopped dried apricots or sultanas.*

Energy 298kcal/1252kJ; Fat 5.2g; Saturated fat 1.4g; Carbohydrate 54.3g; Fibre 0g.

Energy 196kcal/822kJ; Fat 6.6g; Saturated fat 2.27g; Carbohydrate 31.8g; Fibre 0.8g.

Fruit Vermicelli Pudding

This tasty dessert is prepared by Muslims early in the morning of Eid-ul-Fitr, the feast after the 30 days of Ramadan.

Serves 4–6
75g/3oz/6 tbsp ghee
115g/4oz/1 cup Indian vermicelli, coarsely broken
25g/1oz/¼ cup flaked (sliced) almonds
25g/1oz/¼ cup pistachio nuts, slivered
25g/1oz/¼ cup cuddapah nuts or almonds
50g/2oz/⅓ cup sultanas (golden raisins)
50g/2oz/⅓ cup dates, stoned (pitted) and thinly sliced
1.2 litres/2 pints/5 cups full cream (whole) milk
60ml/4 tbsp soft dark brown sugar
1 sachet saffron powder

1 Heat 50g/2oz/4 tbsp of the ghee in a frying pan and sauté the vermicelli until golden brown. (If you are using the Italian variety, sauté it for a little longer.) Remove and set aside.

2 Heat the remaining ghee in a separate pan and fry the almonds, pistachio and cuddapah nuts, sultanas and dates over a medium heat until the sultanas swell. Add the nuts and fruit to the vermicelli and mix gently.

3 Heat the milk in a large, heavy pan and add the sugar. Bring to the boil, add the vermicelli mixture and let the liquid return to the boil, stirring constantly.

4 Reduce the heat and simmer until the vermicelli is soft and you have a fairly thick pudding. Stir in the saffron powder and cook for 1 minute more. Serve hot or cold.

> **Cook's Tip**
> *Cuddapah nuts taste a little like a combination of almonds and pistachio nuts and are also known as almondettes. If you can't locate them use extra almonds for this dish.*

Tapioca Pudding

This pudding, made from large pearl tapioca and coconut milk and served warm, is much lighter than the Western-style version. You can adjust the sweetness to your taste. Serve with lychees, or you could try the smaller, similar-tasting logans.

Serves 4
115g/4oz/⅔ cup tapioca
475ml/16fl oz/2 cups water
175g/6oz/¾ cup granulated sugar
pinch of salt
250ml/8fl oz/1 cup coconut milk
250g/9oz prepared tropical fruits
finely shredded rind of 1 lime, to decorate

1 Soak the tapioca in warm water for 1 hour so that the grains swell. Drain.

2 Put the measured water in a pan and bring to the boil. Stir in the sugar and salt.

3 Add the tapioca and coconut milk and simmer for 10 minutes or until the tapioca turns transparent.

4 Serve warm with some tropical fruits and decorate with the finely shredded lime rind.

> **Cook's Tip**
> *Sliced kiwi fruits, mangoes and strawberries would make a bright and tasty selection to serve with this pudding. Or you could try sliced bananas, nectarines and raspberries.*

> **Variation**
> *Serve this tapioca pudding with a refreshing peach salad for a change. Peel, stone (pit) and very thinly slice 8 peaches and put them in a serving bowl. Add 30ml/2 tbsp rose water, 20ml/4 tsp sugar, the juice of 1 lemon and 50ml/2fl oz/¼ cup freshly squeezed orange juice. Chill well before serving.*

Energy 327kcal/1388kJ; Fat 0.6g; Saturated fat 0.2g; Carbohydrate 80.6g; Fibre 2.2g.

Energy 732kcal/3043kJ; Fat 44.6g; Saturated fat 23.6g; Carbohydrate 68.3g; Fibre 1.7g.

Kulfi with Cardamom

The delicious, traditional Indian ice cream, kulfi, is always made with sweetened full cream milk and is a lovely refreshing way to end an Indian meal. Making kulfi is easy if you use yogurt pots or dariole moulds.

Serves 6
2 litres/3 ½ pints/9 cups creamy milk
12 cardamoms
175g/6oz/scant 1 cup caster (superfine) sugar
25g/1oz/¼ cup blanched almonds, chopped
toasted flaked (sliced) almonds and cardamoms, to decorate

1 Place the milk and cardamom pods in a large, heavy pan. Bring to the boil then simmer vigorously until reduced by one-third.

2 Strain the milk into a bowl, discarding the cardamoms, then stir in the caster sugar and chopped almonds until the sugar is dissolved. Leave to cool.

3 Pour the mixture into a freezerproof container, cover and freeze until almost firm, stirring every 30 minutes.

4 When almost solid, pack the ice cream into six kulfi moulds or clean yogurt pots. Return to the freezer until required, removing the pots about 10 minutes before serving and turning out the individual ices. Decorate with toasted almonds and cardamoms before serving.

> **Variation**
> Rose water is also a traditional flavouring for kulfi. Add 15ml/ 1 tbsp to the recipe, if you like.

> **Cook's Tip**
> Use a large pan for reducing the milk as there needs to be plenty of room for it to bubble up.

Leche Flan

Serve this delicious dessert hot or cold, with whipped cream or crème fraîche.

Serves 8
5 large eggs
30ml/2 tbsp caster (superfine) sugar
few drops vanilla extract
400g/14oz can evaporated (unsweetened condensed) milk
300ml/½ pint/1 ¼ cups milk
5ml/1 tsp finely grated lime rind
strips of lime rind, to decorate

For the caramel
225g/8oz/generous 1 cup sugar
120ml/4fl oz/½ cup water

1 To make the caramel, put the sugar and water in a heavy pan. Stir to dissolve the sugar, then boil without stirring until the caramel is golden.

2 Quickly pour into eight individual ramekins, rotating them to coat the sides. Leave to one side to set.

3 Preheat the oven to 150°C/300°F/Gas 2. Beat the eggs, sugar and vanilla extract in a bowl.

4 Mix the evaporated milk and fresh milk in a pan. Heat to just below boiling point, then pour on to the egg mixture, stirring all the time. Strain the custard mixture into a jug (pitcher) and add the grated lime rind. Leave the custard to cool. Pour into the caramel-coated ramekins.

5 Place the ramekins in a roasting pan and pour in enough warm water to come halfway up the sides of the dishes.

6 Transfer the roasting pan to the oven and cook the custards for 35–45 minutes or until just set. They will just shimmer when the ramekins are gently shaken.

7 Serve the custards in their ramekin dishes. Alternatively, invert them on to serving plates. Break up the caramel into smaller pieces and use to decorate the custards. The custards can be served warm or cold, decorated with strips of lime rind.

Energy 401kcal/1686kJ; Fat 19.3g; Saturated fat 11.2g; Carbohydrate 46.8g; Fibre 0.3g.

Energy 229kcal/967kJ; Fat 6.2g; Saturated fat 2.7g; Carbohydrate 36.4g; Fibre 0g.

Caramel Custard with Fresh Fruit

A creamy caramel dessert is a wonderful way to end a meal. It is light and delicious, and this recipe is very simple to make. Fresh fruit is the perfect accompaniment.

Serves 6
30ml/2 tbsp granulated sugar
30ml/2 tbsp water

For the custard
6 eggs
4 drops vanilla extract
115g/4oz/generous ½ cup
   granulated sugar
750ml/1¼ pints/3 cups
   semi-skimmed (low-fat) milk
fresh fruit, such as strawberries,
   blueberries, orange and banana
   slices, and raspberries, to serve

1 To make the caramel, place the sugar and water in a heavy pan and heat until the sugar has dissolved and the mixture is bubbling and pale gold in colour. Watch the sugar carefully, as it can quickly burn once it begins to caramelize. Pour carefully into a 1.2 litre/2 pint/5 cup soufflé dish. Leave the caramel to cool.

2 Preheat the oven to 180°C/350°F/Gas 4. To make the custard, break the eggs into a medium mixing bowl and whisk until frothy.

3 Stir the vanilla extract into the whisked eggs and gradually add the granulated sugar. Add the milk in a steady stream, whisking constantly.

4 Pour the custard over the top of the caramel.

5 Cook the custard in the oven for 35–40 minutes. Remove from the oven and leave to cool for 30 minutes or until the mixture is set.

6 Loosen the custard from the sides of the dish with a knife. Place a serving dish upside-down on top of the soufflé dish and invert, giving a gentle shake if necessary to turn out the custard on to the serving dish.

7 Arrange any fresh fruit of your choice around the custard on the serving dish and serve immediately.

Energy 194kcal/823kJ; Fat 4.7g; Saturated fat 2.01g; Carbohydrate 32.9g; Fibre 0g.

Coconut Cream Diamonds

Although commercially ground rice can be used for this dish, grinding jasmine rice yourself – in a food processor – gives a much better result.

Serves 4–6
75g/3oz/scant ½ cup jasmine
   rice, soaked overnight in
   175ml/6fl oz/¾ cup water
350ml/12fl oz/1½ cups
   coconut milk
150ml/¼ pint/⅔ cup single
   (light) cream

50g/2oz/¼ cup caster
   (superfine) sugar
raspberries and fresh mint leaves,
   to decorate

For the coulis
75g/3oz/¾ cup blackcurrants,
   stalks removed
30ml/2 tbsp caster
   (superfine) sugar
75g/3oz/½ cup fresh or
   frozen raspberries

1 Put the rice and its soaking water into a food processor and process for a few minutes until the mixture is soupy. Heat the coconut milk and cream in a non-stick pan. When the mixture is on the point of boiling, stir in the rice mixture. Cook over a very gentle heat for 10 minutes, stirring constantly.

2 Stir the sugar into the coconut rice mixture and continue cooking for a further 10–15 minutes, or until the mixture is thick and creamy. Line a rectangular tin (pan) with baking parchment. Pour the coconut rice mixture into the pan, cool, then chill until the dessert is set and firm.

3 To make the coulis, put the blackcurrants in a bowl and sprinkle with the sugar. Set aside for 30 minutes. Transfer the blackcurrants and raspberries to a sieve (strainer) over a bowl. Using a spoon, press the fruit against the sieve so that the juices collect in the bowl. Taste the coulis and add more sugar if necessary.

4 Cut the coconut cream into diamonds. Spoon a little of the coulis on to each plate, arrange the diamonds on top and decorate with the raspberries and mint leaves.

Energy 248kcal/1043kJ; Fat 7.8g; Saturated fat 4.8g; Carbohydrate 42.2g; Fibre 1.2g.

Coconut Custard

This traditional dessert can be baked or steamed and is often served with sweet sticky rice and a selection of fresh fruit. Mangoes and tamarillos go particularly well with the custard and rice. Rose or jasmine extract give the custard a distinctive flavour but vanilla also works well.

Serves 4
4 eggs
75g/3oz/6 tbsp soft light brown sugar
250ml/8fl oz/1 cup coconut milk
5ml/1 tsp vanilla, rose or jasmine extract
fresh mint leaves and icing (confectioners') sugar, to decorate
sliced fruit, to serve

1 Preheat the oven to 150°C/300°F/Gas 2.

2 Whisk the eggs and sugar in a bowl until smooth. Add the coconut milk and the vanilla, rose or jasmine extract and whisk well.

3 Strain the mixture into a jug (pitcher), then pour it into four individual heatproof glasses, ramekins or an ovenproof dish.

4 Stand the glasses, ramekins or dish in a roasting pan.

5 Fill the pan with hot water to reach halfway up the sides of the ramekins or dish.

6 Bake for about 35–40 minutes, or until the custards are set. Test with a fine skewer or cocktail stick (toothpick).

7 Remove the roasting pan from the oven, lift out the ramekins or dish and leave to cool.

8 If you like, turn out the custards on to a serving plate or plates. Decorate with the mint leaves and a dusting of icing sugar, and serve with sliced fruit such as ripe peaches, mangoes, papaya, star fruit (carambola) or kiwi fruit.

Mango & Lime Fool

Canned mangoes are used here for convenience, but the dish tastes even better if made with fresh ones. Choose a variety such as the voluptuous Alphonso mango, which is wonderfully fragrant and also tastes indescribably delicious.

Serves 4
400g/14oz can sliced mango
grated rind of 1 lime
juice of ½ lime
150ml/¼ pint/⅔ cup double (heavy) cream
90ml/6 tbsp Greek (US strained plain) yogurt
fresh mango slices, to decorate (optional)

1 Drain the canned mango slices and put them in the bowl of a food processor.

2 Add the grated lime rind and the lime juice. Process until the mixture forms a smooth purée. Alternatively, mash the mango slices with a potato masher, then press through a sieve (strainer) into a bowl with the back of a wooden spoon. Stir in the lime rind and juice.

3 Pour the cream into a bowl and add the yogurt. Whisk until the mixture is thick and then quickly whisk in the mango mixture.

4 Spoon into four tall cups or glasses and chill for 1–2 hours. Just before serving, decorate each glass with fresh mango slices, if you like.

> **Cook's Tip**
> *When mixing the cream and yogurt mixture with the mango purée, whisk just enough to combine, so as not to lose the lightness of the whipped cream mixture. If you prefer, fold the mixtures together lightly, so that the fool is rippled.*

Energy 269kcal/1118kJ; Fat 22.6g; Saturated fat 13.8g; Carbohydrate 15.2g; Fibre 2.6g.

Energy 161kcal/681kJ; Fat 5.7g; Saturated fat 1.7g; Carbohydrate 22.7g; Fibre 0g.

Mango Sorbet with Sauce

After a heavy meal, this delightful sorbet makes a very refreshing dessert. Mango is said to be one of the oldest fruits cultivated in India, having been presented by Lord Shiva to his beautiful wife, Parvathi.

Serves 4–6
900g/2lb mango pulp
2.5ml/1/2 tsp lemon juice
grated rind of 1 orange and
    1 lemon

4 egg whites
50g/2oz/1/4 cup caster
    (superfine) sugar
120ml/4fl oz/1/2 cup double
    (heavy) cream
50g/2oz/1/2 cup icing
    (confectioners') sugar

1 In a large, chilled bowl, mix half of the mango pulp with the lemon juice and the grated rind.

2 Whisk the egg whites until peaks form, then gently fold them into the mango mixture, with the caster sugar. Cover with clear film (plastic wrap) and place in the freezer for at least 1 hour.

3 Remove from the freezer and beat again. Transfer to an ice cream container, and freeze until fully set.

4 In a bowl, whip the double cream with the icing sugar and the remaining mango pulp. Cover and chill the sauce for 24 hours.

5 Remove the sorbet 10 minutes before serving. Scoop out individual servings and cover with a generous helping of mango sauce. Serve immediately.

Variation
Try this sorbet made with full-flavoured locally grown strawberries when in season for a delicious change.

Indian Ice Cream

Kulfi-wallahs (ice-cream vendors) have always made kulfi, and continue to this day, without using modern freezers. Kulfi is packed into metal cones sealed with dough and then churned in clay pots until set. Try this method – it works extremely well in an ordinary freezer.

350g/12oz/3 cups icing
    (confectioners') sugar
5ml/1 tsp ground cardamom
15ml/1 tbsp rose water
175g/6oz/1 1/2 cups pistachio
    nuts, chopped
75g/3oz/1/2 cup sultanas
    (golden raisins)
75g/3oz/3/4 cup flaked
    (sliced) almonds
25g/1oz/3 tbsp glacé (candied)
    cherries, halved

Serves 4–6
3 × 400ml/14fl oz cans
    evaporated (unsweetened
    condensed) milk
3 egg whites

1 Remove the labels from the cans of evaporated milk and lay the cans down in a pan with a tight-fitting cover. Fill the pan with water to reach three-quarters up the cans. Bring to the boil, cover and simmer for 20 minutes. (Don't leave the cans of evaporated milk unattended. Top up the water if necessary; the pan must never boil dry.) When cool, remove the cans and chill in the refrigerator for 24 hours. Chill a large bowl too.

2 Whisk the egg whites in another large bowl until peaks form. Open the cans and empty the milk into the chilled bowl. Whisk until doubled in quantity, then fold in the whisked egg whites and icing sugar.

3 Gently fold in the remaining ingredients, cover the bowl with clear film (plastic wrap) and place in the freezer for 1 hour.

4 Remove the ice cream from the freezer and mix well with a fork. Transfer to a serving container and return to the freezer for a final setting. Remove from the freezer 10 minutes before serving.

Coconut & Lemon Grass Ice Cream

The combination of cream and coconut milk makes for a wonderfully rich ice cream. The lemon grass flavouring is very subtle, but quite delicious.

Serves 4
2 lemon grass stalks
475ml/16fl oz/2 cups double
    (heavy) cream
120ml/4fl oz/½ cup coconut
    milk
4 large (US extra large) eggs
105ml/7 tbsp caster
    (superfine) sugar
5ml/1 tsp vanilla extract

1 Cut the lemon grass stalks in half lengthways. Use a mallet or rolling pin to mash the pieces, breaking up the fibres so that all the flavour is released. Pour the cream and coconut milk into a pan. Add the lemon grass stalks and heat gently, stirring frequently, until the mixture starts to simmer.

2 Put the eggs, sugar and vanilla extract in a large bowl. Using an electric whisk, whisk until the mixture is very light and fluffy.

3 Strain the cream mixture into a heatproof bowl that will fit over a pan of simmering water. Whisk in the egg mixture, then place the bowl over the pan and continue to whisk until the mixture thickens. Remove it from the heat and leave to cool. Chill the coconut custard in the refrigerator for 3–4 hours.

4 Pour the mixture into a plastic tub or similar freezerproof container. Freeze for 4 hours, beating two or three times at hourly intervals with a fork to break up the ice crystals.

5 Alternatively, use an ice-cream maker. Pour the chilled mixture into the machine and churn until it is firm enough to scoop. Serve immediately, or scrape into a freezerproof container and place in the freezer. Allow the ice cream to soften in the refrigerator for 30 minutes before serving.

Energy 773kcal/3200kJ; Fat 69.4g; Saturated fat 41.3g; Carbohydrate 30.9g; Fibre 0g.

Coconut Ice Cream

This ice cream is easy to make in an ice-cream maker or by hand. Serve it with a spicy *gula melaka* sauce, hot, warm or cold.

Serves 6
400ml/14fl oz can coconut milk
400ml/14fl oz can condensed
    milk
2.5ml/½ tsp salt

For the gula melaka *sauce*
150g/5oz/¾ cup palm sugar
    or muscovado (molasses)
    sugar
150ml/¼ pint/⅔ cup water
1cm/½in slice fresh root
    ginger, bruised
1 pandanus leaf (if available)
coconut shells (optional) and
    thinly pared strips of coconut,
    to serve

1 Chill the cans of coconut and condensed milk thoroughly. In a bowl, mix the coconut milk with the condensed milk. Gently whisk together with the salt.

2 Pour the mixture into the frozen freezer bowl of an ice-cream maker (or follow the appliance instructions) and churn until thickened. (This will take 30–40 minutes.) Transfer the mixture to a lidded plastic tub, cover and freeze until the consistency is right for scooping.

3 If you do not have an ice-cream maker, pour the mixture into a shallow container and freeze on the coldest setting. When ice crystals form around the sides of the ice cream, beat the mixture, then return it to the freezer. Do this at least twice. The more you do it, the creamier the mixture will be.

4 To make the sauce, mix the sugar, measured water and ginger in a pan. Stir over medium heat until the sugar has dissolved, then bring the liquid to the boil. Add the pandanus leaf, if using, tying it into a knot so that it can easily be removed with the ginger before serving. Lower the heat and simmer for 3–4 minutes. Set aside until required.

5 Serve the ice cream in coconut shells or a bowl. Decorate with coconut and serve with the hot, warm or cold sauce.

Energy 237kcal/1001kJ; Fat 6.9g; Saturated fat 4.3g; Carbohydrate 40.3g; Fibre 0g.

Watermelon Ice

After a hot and spicy meal, the only thing more refreshing than ice-cold watermelon is this cooling watermelon ice. Making it is simplicity itself.

4 kaffir lime leaves, torn into small pieces
500g/1lb watermelon

Serves 4–6
90ml/6 tbsp caster (superfine) sugar
105ml/7 tbsp water

1 Put the caster sugar, water and kaffir lime leaves in a pan. Heat gently until the sugar has dissolved. Pour into a large bowl and set aside to cool.

2 Cut the watermelon into wedges with a large knife. Cut the flesh from the rind, remove the seeds and chop the flesh.

3 Spoon the watermelon into a food processor. Process to a slush, then mix with the sugar syrup. Chill the mixture in the refrigerator for 3–4 hours.

4 Strain the mixture into a freezerproof container. Freeze for 2 hours, then remove from the freezer and beat with a fork to break up the ice crystals. Return the mixture to the freezer and freeze for 3 hours more, beating the mixture at half-hourly intervals. Freeze until firm.

5 Alternatively, use an ice-cream maker. Pour the chilled mixture into the machine and churn until it is firm enough to scoop. Serve immediately, or scrape into a freezerproof container and store in the freezer.

6 About 30 minutes before serving, transfer the watermelon ice to the refrigerator so that it softens slightly. This allows the full flavour of the watermelon to be apparent and makes the ice easier to scoop.

Spiced Lassi

Lassi, or buttermilk, is prepared by churning yogurt with water and then removing the fat. To make this refreshing drink without churning, use low-fat natural yogurt instead.

Serves 4
450ml/¾ pint/scant 2 cups natural (plain) yogurt

300ml/½ pint/1¼ cups water
2.5cm/1in piece fresh root ginger, finely crushed
2 fresh green chillies, finely chopped
2.5ml/½ tsp ground cumin
salt and ground black pepper
a few fresh coriander (cilantro) leaves, chopped, to garnish

1 In a bowl, whisk the yogurt and water until well blended. The consistency should be that of full cream (whole) milk. Adjust by adding more water if necessary.

2 Add the ginger, chillies and ground cumin.

3 Season with the salt and black pepper, and mix well.

4 Pour into four serving glasses and chill. Garnish with chopped coriander before serving.

Cook's Tip
Lassi is often drunk with hot and spicy curries as it refreshes the palate well.

Variation
If you prefer an unspiced and cooler version, try Rose Water Lassi. Blend 300ml/½ pint/1¼ cups natural yogurt with 60ml/4 tbsp caster sugar, 400ml/14fl oz/1⅔ cups water and 15ml/1 tbsp rose water in a food processor or blender. Pour into individual glasses or a jug (pitcher) and add fresh mint leaves to decorate, if you like.

Energy 128kcal/545kJ; Fat 0.4g; Saturated fat 0.1g; Carbohydrate 32.4g; Fibre 0.1g.

Energy 63kcal/266kJ; Fat 1.1g; Saturated fat 0.6g; Carbohydrate 8.5g; Fibre 0g.

Pistachio Lassi

In India, lassi is not only made at home, but is also sold at roadside cafés, restaurants and hotels. There is no substitute for this drink, especially on a hot day. It is particularly good served with curries and similar hot dishes as it helps the body to digest spicy food.

Serves 4
300ml/ ½ pint/1 ¼ cups natural (plain) low-fat yogurt
5ml/1 tsp granulated sugar, or to taste
300ml/ ½ pint/1 ¼ cups water
30ml/2 tbsp puréed fruit (optional)
15ml/1 tbsp crushed pistachio nuts, to decorate

1 Place the natural yogurt in a jug (pitcher) and whisk until frothy. Add the granulated sugar.

2 Pour in the measured water and the puréed fruit, if using, and continue to whisk for 2 minutes.

3 Taste for sweetness and adjust as necessary. Pour the lassi into four serving glasses and serve chilled, decorated with crushed pistachio nuts.

Cook's Tips
• Refreshing, cooling drinks are the perfect accompaniment to spicy Indian dishes.
• A variety of fruit juices are often served as well as water flavoured with freshly squeezed limes or lemons and sweetened with sugar. Fresh fragrant mint is usually used to decorate and flavour the drinks.

Variation
To make a simple savoury lassi, omit the sugar and fruit and add lemon juice, ground cumin and salt. Garnish with fresh mint leaves.

Tea & Fruit Punch

This delicious punch can be served hot or cold. White wine or brandy may be added to taste.

Makes 4
600ml/1 pint/2½ cups water
1 cinnamon stick
4 cloves
12.5ml/2 ½ tsp Earl Grey tea leaves
175g/6oz/scant 1 cup granulated sugar
450ml/¾ pint/scant 2 cups tropical soft drink concentrate
1 lemon, sliced
1 small orange, sliced
½ cucumber, sliced

1 Bring the water to the boil in a pan with the cinnamon stick and cloves. Remove from the heat and add the tea leaves. Leave to brew for about 5 minutes. Stir and strain into a large bowl and chill in the refrigerator for 2–3 hours.

2 Add the sugar and the soft drink concentrate and allow to rest until the sugar has dissolved and the mixture cooled. Place the fruit and cucumber in a chilled punch bowl and pour over the tea mix. Chill for a further 24 hours before serving.

Almond Sherbet

Traditionally, this drink was always made in the month of Ramadan to break the Muslim fast. It should be served chilled.

Serves 4
50g/2oz/½ cup ground almonds
600ml/1 pint/2½ cups semi-skimmed (low-fat) milk
10ml/2 tsp granulated sugar, or to taste

1 Put the ground almonds into a serving jug (pitcher).

2 Pour in the semi-skimmed milk and add the sugar; stir to mix.

3 Taste for sweetness and adjust as necessary. Serve very cold in long glasses. Chilling the glasses first helps to keep the drink cold and adds a sense of occasion.

Energy 70kcal/296kJ; Fat 2.6g; Saturated fat 0.63g; Carbohydrate 7.5g; Fibre 0g.

Top: Energy 1108kcal/4737kJ; Fat 0g; Saturated fat 0g; Carbohydrate 294.5g; Fibre 0g;
Above: Energy 155kcal/651kJ; Fat 9.4g; Saturated fat 2.04g; Carbohydrate 11g; Fibre 0.9g.

Index